Majestic Lights
The Apostle Islands Lighthouses

By Jim Merkel

JCM Press
4216 Osceola St.
St. Louis, MO 63116

Majestic Lights
The Apostle Islands Lighthouses

Copyright 2001 by Jim Merkel. All rights reserved.
Many thanks to Donna Chilton, Mary Ann Hartzell and Aristotle Kumpis of Graphics Associates, Inc., St. Louis, MO for a fine job of designing and printing this book.

Quotations from *The Lake Superior Country In History and In Story*, by Guy M. Burnham, used by permission of Paradigm Press, P.O. Box 123, Ashland, WI 54806.

The chapters on the six light stations of the Apostle Islands National Lakeshore, the Lake Superior Big Top Chautauqua, Randall J. Peterson, the Apostle Islands Lighthouse Celebration and The Heart of a Keeper are revised and updated versions of articles published in the international monthly lighthouse magazine *Lighthouse Digest* in 1998, 1999 and 2000. Used by permission.

Quotations from the 1931 article by Stella Champney used in the chapter on the Michigan Island Light Station are reprinted with permission from *The Detroit News*.

Unless otherwise noted, photographs are by the author. Aerial photo of Ashland Harbor Breakwater Light on the back cover and inside is by Marvin Aerial Photography. Prints may be purchased at MAP, P.O. Box 74, Addison, MI 49220, or www.greatlakeslighthouses.com.

Copyrighted illustrations of Apostle Islands Light Stations by Randall J. Peterson are used by permission of Randall Peterson Designs, 625 Schilling Circle NW, Forest Lake, MN 55025.

Historic photos are provided courtesy the Apostle Islands National Lakeshore. The Apostle Islands National Lakeshore also provided current photos of the LaPointe and Chequamegon Point lights.

Drawings came from a building survey done from 1989-91 by the Historic American Buildings Survey/Historic American Engineering Record Division of the National Park Service (HABS/HAER) and the Apostle Islands National Lakeshore. Each drawing is identified (HABS/HAER) with the year it was made.

I am the light of the world; he that followeth me shall not walk in darkness, but shall have the light of life.
John 8:12
Bible quotations are from the King James Version.

ISBN 0-9710062-0-2

Table of Contents

Notes to Readers

This book refers frequently to the Fresnel lens, which was developed by the French physicist Augustin Jean Fresnel (1788-1827). Shaped generally like a globe, this highly-efficient series of compound lenses encloses the light source and aims parallel beams in one direction. There are seven "orders" of size, from one to six, with an extra $3^1/_2$ Order. In general, a 1st Order lens is the biggest and most powerful and a 6th Order lens is least powerful and smallest.

Those who do not pronounce the "s" in "Fresnel" will be on their way to becoming 1st Order experts on lighthouses.

The Apostle Islands lighthouse figurines by Kim Bloomquist on the front cover are, left to right, old Michigan Island Lighthouse, Sand Island Lighthouse, Chequamegon Point Light, Outer Island Lighthouse, Devils Island Light tower, Ashland Harbor Breakwater Light and Raspberry Island Lighthouse. The figurines are used by permission of Keeper of the Light lighthouse and nautical gift store, Bayfield, Wisc., which sells them in its store.

Before taking the front cover photograph, St. Louis, Mo. newspaper photographer Dennis Caldwell laid the figurines on top of a National Oceanic and Atmospheric Administration navigational chart of the Apostle Islands region. Caldwell also did the inside photo preparation.

On the back cover are pictures of the eight light towers of the Apostle Islands National Lakeshore, plus the Ashland Harbor Breakwater Light. The other photos and illustrations on the back cover can be found in the pages of this book.

In many older works, the name of the location of the northernmost light station in Wisconsin is spelled "Devil's Island." However, in the most common spelling today, there is no apostrophe. Except in direct quotations from writings that use the older form, the modern spelling, Devils Island, is used herein.

Also, the name of the village at the west end of Madeline Island and one name of the light station on Long Island is variously spelled La Pointe and LaPointe. This book uses the more popular spelling, LaPointe.

Introduction

In 1995, I was paging through some travel books when I came across this neat collection of islands in Lake Superior. There, you could take a ferry across to a cute little town on one of those islands, and drive over in the winter when the lake froze. There were plenty of lighthouses to see and any number of other things to do. Excitedly, my wife and I drove north to Bayfield, Wisc., expecting to have the second best vacation of our marriage – after our honeymoon, of course. We couldn't think of a better way to get away from the heat of St. Louis.

As others who have visited the place can relate, we weren't disappointed. This journalist didn't need an investigative travel reporter from the *Chicago Tribune* to tell him Bayfield is the Best Little Town in the Midwest. I could have told him that.

If I'd merely found a place for us to go on our weeks off from work, it would have been enough. But I found a new love for lighthouses.

These led me to start writing a novel based on one lighthouse in the Apostles and to write regularly for the international monthly lighthouse magazine, *Lighthouse Digest*. This book grew from a series of articles I did for *Lighthouse Digest* on the Apostle Islands lighthouses. The title of this book, by the way, is taken from my novel's name for the archipelago in Lake Superior just off Wisconsin: the Majestic Islands. (You say they aren't majestic?) It is my hope that readers will find this a quick, thorough, accurate and entertaining look at the premier collection of lighthouses in the National Park System.

This little volume includes chapters about each of the light stations, along with one station's log for several years, recollections of lighthouse people in their own words and the story of the longest-serving lighthouse family in the Apostles. Other chapters tell about an annual gathering of lighthouse people in the Apostles and a production about the lighthouses by a local theatrical group.

There also is a chapter about the Ashland Harbor Breakwater Light. This lighthouse that welcomes vessels to the city of Ashland is not in the Apostle Islands and often is left out of discussions about the lighthouses of the area. However, it is part of the overall system of navigation aids that direct shipping into the area. It is as much a member of the Apostle Islands region group of lighthouses as any of the other six lighthouses.

The book ends with a personal touch. I have included a short story from my novel. An afterword gives the reasons I believe lighthouses are so popular. Beware, though, lest your love for lights grow into fanaticism. Your friends and relatives will give you nothing but lighthouse calendars and towels for Christmas.

I wish to acknowledge the help of a number of people who made this book possible. Foremost among them is Bob Mackreth, historian for the Apostle Islands National Lakeshore. He spent a generous amount of time with the author, and provided him with much information and many of the quotes printed herein. Jim Nepstad, management assistant at the National Lakeshore, also offered valuable help.

Tim Harrison and Kathleen Finnegan of *Lighthouse Digest* magazine; Mary Grant of Keeper of the Light gift and book shop; Dave Strzok of the Apostle Islands Cruise Service; and John Teeter of Bayfield Street Publishing also deserve several free lunches for the help they provided.

Dennis Caldwell, chief photographer for the newspaper that pays my salary, did a sterling job with the cover photo work and in turning my pictures into something usable. He is the mountain lover I mention in the afterword. Jack Cowan, our paper's chief copy editor, also pitched in with copyediting and taking out extra commas.

Others I can't forget are Lois Spangle; Bob Parker; the Wiinamakis; Jeanne and Mike Goodier of the Seagull Bay Motel, for the rooms with a view; Warren Nelson; my brother, Charles; NiNi Harris; my boss, Jim Rygelski; and the friends, co-workers and relatives who tolerate my obsession.

Most of all, I want to thank my wife, Lorraine. Thanks, honey, for all the proofreading you did and the many days and nights you've allowed me to work on my lighthouse writing projects. No matter how good lighthouses get, you outshine them all.

Jim Merkel
March 2001

Chapter One

The Place for Lighthouses: The Apostle Islands Region

Americans love lighthouses, but cannot always name them. Many of them, though, keep pictures in their minds of lights at famous places like Cape Hatteras in North Carolina, West Quoddy Head in Maine or Point Reyes in California.

Relatively few will be able to name or picture the Sand Island or Raspberry Island lighthouses, or the other lighthouses in the Apostle Islands region of Lake Superior. When they learn those lights are in Wisconsin, some might say, "Aren't they in Door County?"

No, they're not. They are at the very top of Wisconsin, at a destination not easy to find. To view those lights, travelers must come to the town of Bayfield, 220 miles from Minneapolis-St. Paul, 370 miles from Milwaukee and 465 miles from Chicago.

The nearest airport with scheduled flights is in Duluth, ninety miles away. The best way to drive from the south is along narrow U.S. Highway 51, through crowded tourist destinations like Minocqua.

It's not easy to get to the little town along Wisconsin Highway 13. But for lovers of lighthouses, the trip to Bayfield and the Apostle Islands is worth taking. For here, within an afternoon's boat ride, are seven distinctively different, formerly manned light stations with a total of nine towers and the ruins of a tenth.

"The Apostle Islands, the Apostle Islands area and the Apostle Islands National Lakeshore is probably as far as I'm concerned the holy grail of lighthouse aficionados," said Bob Mackreth, historian for the Apostle Islands National Lakeshore. "It is for the National Park Service the premier collection of lighthouses in any one area."

A former National Park ranger who took twenty years to get into his chosen field of history, Mackreth said he's the luckiest man in the world for having his job.

"I challenge people to point to anywhere else in the country where you have such a wide variety of lighthouses with such a diverse history in such a small compact area," Mackreth told a group at the Apostle Islands Lighthouse Celebration in 1998.

The six light stations within the Apostle Islands National Lakeshore were built from 1857 to 1891 to provide directions for vessels serving first the old French fur trading village of LaPointe and later the bustling port towns of Bayfield, Washburn and Ashland. The lights on the edge of the Apostles, at Sand, Devils and Outer islands, had the added duty of serving traffic to and from Duluth and Superior, at the lake's far western end.

Any complete telling of the story of those six light stations should include details about a seventh. The Ashland Harbor Breakwater Light is not physically within the Apostles or the National Lakeshore and normally is not a part of guides to the islands' lighthouses. It is not an Apostle Islands lighthouse. But this light station at the south end of Chequamegon Bay – first illuminated in 1911 – marked the end point of a trip that brought vessels past other lights of the archipelago. The seven light stations should be considered together, as lights of the Apostle Islands region.

The new communities the Apostle Islands lighthouses guarded grew up after the opening of the first of the Sault Ste. Marie Canals in 1855. The new waterways between Lake Superior and Lake Huron, also called the "Soo Canals," enabled ships to get around the rapids in the natural connection between the two lakes, the St. Marys River.

The world now had a highway into a previously isolated area of North America. As with any highway, this one needed street lights. New lighthouses that served that purpose sprang up throughout Lake Superior, including in the Apostles.

The steamers and freighters kept coming, increasing the need for vigilance among lighthouse keepers.

"The port of Ashland carried about three times as much cargo tonnage per season as the combined New York State canals," local writer Guy Burnham wrote, speaking of the 1923 shipping season. In his book, *The Lake Superior Country in History and in Story*, Burnham included statistics that showed more tons of cargo moved in and out of Ashland in 1925 than any other Wisconsin port, including Milwaukee.

The decline in the number of ore boats, coal boats and pulpwood rafts coming into the region helped end the area's status as a large stopping-off point for shipping, and left Duluth and Superior as the major international ports serving the northwestern end of the Great Lakes.

Meanwhile, new technology made it increasingly unnecessary to have keepers at illuminated navigational aids. The path of progress began in the Apostles in 1921, with the automation of the Sand Island Light Station. The era of keepers ended in the island group in 1978, when a five-person U.S. Coast Guard crew left the station at Devils Island.

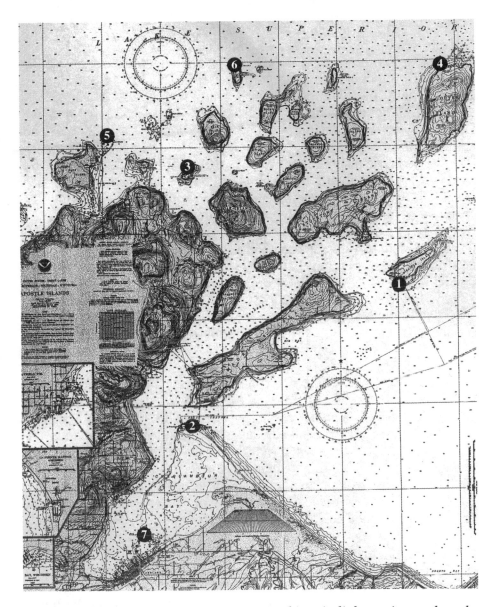

The Apostle Islands region contains seven historic light stations, when the Ashland Harbor Breakwater Light is added to the six stations of the Apostle Islands National Lakeshore. Five of the stations each have one tower. Michigan Island has two towers, while Long Island (LaPointe) has two towers and the ruins of the original tower. The locations of each station is shown in this reduced-size copy of a navigational chart of the Apostle Islands area. The stations, in order of when they were first lit, are:

1) Michigan Island (1857)
2) Long Island (LaPointe) (1858)
3) Raspberry Island (1863)
4) Outer Island (1874)
5) Sand Island (1881)
6) Devils Island (1891)
7) Ashland Harbor Breakwater (1911)

The port trade and the keepers are gone, but not the travelers who come to see the Apostles and its lighthouses.

Interest in preservation of the historical and natural treasures of the area led to the creation of the Apostle Islands National Lakeshore in 1970. Initially, the lakeshore included all but two of the Apostle Islands and the lighthouses at Sand, Devils, Outer, Raspberry and Michigan islands. Later, Long Island was added and with it the LaPointe and Chequamegon Point Lights.

Today, the lakeshore has twelve miles of mainland shoreline and twenty one of the twenty two Apostle Islands. It is filled with isolated sand beaches, bits of remaining old growth forest, breathtaking sea caves and lighthouses. Each year, about 200,000 people visit the lakeshore to camp, spot a black bear or an eagle, take a cruise through the islands and learn more about light stations.

Many make their base in Bayfield, a town filled with historic Queen Anne - style homes that brags it kept out fast food restaurants. Adding to the attractions is the village of LaPointe on Madeline Island, a two-and-a-half-mile-long ferry ride from Bayfield; and the locally-produced historical plays at the Lake Superior Big Top Chautauqua.

Chicago Tribune reporter Alan Solomon discovered the pull in 1997, on a six-week tour of 139 towns in the Midwest. At the end of this dream assignment, he reported to his readers that Bayfield was, for vacationers, the Best Little Town in the Midwest.

Key to this is the role the federal government has played, by designating much of the area a National Lakeshore. With limited funding, the National Park Service has taken significant steps to preserve the treasures of the Apostle Islands and keep them accessible. For lovers of lighthouses, the light stations are at the top of that list of treasures.

"If it were not for the lakeshore, many of these resources would not be maintained," said John Neal, superintendent of the Apostle Islands National Lakeshore, speaking of the lighthouses. "Obviously, they're very expensive to maintain."

In most cases, the light stations are only stabilized, and not restored to any extent, Neal said.

But stabilization in itself is an important part of keeping the lights for future generations. Without erosion control projects at Raspberry and Outer islands, the lights soon would be in jeopardy, officials say.

Under the stewardship of the National Park Service, the Apostle Islands lighthouses are in much better shape than they would be otherwise, said Dave Snyder. He was Mackreth's predecessor as Apostle Islands National Lakeshore historian and now is historian of the U.S. Lighthouse Society.

"The Park Service has really pumped in a lot of money," Snyder said. "I think the Park Service has been really good caretakers of the lighthouses and have kept them in good shape and if they had passed into other hands perhaps they wouldn't be in as good a shape as they are."

If the National Park Service hadn't taken over the lighthouses, they likely would have gone to several different kinds of property owners, Snyder speculates.

The lights on Michigan and Sand islands, which previously were leased to individuals, might have moved into private ownership.

"They could have private property signs and you just wouldn't be able to get out there. And private ownership isn't always bad, because sometimes they turn these into bed and breakfasts," Snyder said. "Sometimes they could have put more money into it than the Park Service could have, but probably you wouldn't have the access that you have today, unless it was a commercial structure like a (bed and breakfast) or something."

The two lights on Long Island might have become part of the nearby reservation of the Bad River Band of Lake Superior Chippewa Indians, Snyder said.

The lights at Outer, Devils or Raspberry islands could have passed into the hands of the state. Or else Bayfield would have acquired them, possibly through the auspices of the Bayfield Heritage Association.

"You've really got a variety of architectural styles, and you've got a nice concentration of lighthouses in one spot, as well as a really awesome natural setting for each of them," Snyder said.

Snyder offered these examples:

- "You've got a lighthouse constructed during the Civil War . . . on Raspberry Island. It looks much like a lighthouse out east, because there aren't that many wooden frame lighthouses on the Great Lakes. . . . It has more of a New England look to it."

- "You've got the stone cookie-cutter lighthouse on Sand Island, the same as like four or five other lighthouses on the Great Lakes, just varying by its composition in sandstone."

- "You've got the two dwellings on Devils Island that are as nice as anything you'd see in Ashland or Duluth in one of the streetcar suburbs. You see these Victorian Queen Anne dwellings. Of course, there you've got a skeletal tower."

Neal looks at the lights as a historian.

"To me they're part of a very fascinating chapter in the history of the islands themselves," he said. "What I like most about the lighthouses besides looking at the structures is learning about the human part of that story, the lightkeepers, their families, the kinds of things that they endured."

No wonder Mackreth could say to the crowd in the auditorium at the Apostle Islands Lighthouse Celebration, "This is the place to come for lighthouses."

Chapter Two
Michigan Island:
The Mistake
That Became a Treasure

As she climbs the stairway of the working light tower of the Michigan Island Light Station, Ann Mahan utters a key statement about the place.

"One of the unique things lighthouse-wise is that it has the two lighthouses," said Mahan, half of a husband-and-wife writing and picture-taking team specializing in the Great Lakes.

In that sentence, Mahan sums up much of the attractiveness of the light station, which contains at the same time the oldest and the newest towers of the six light stations of the Apostle Islands National Lakeshore.

The big story about Michigan Island is the reason there are two light towers on Michigan Island. For here is a subject for an expose on a late 1850s version of *60 Minutes* or *Dateline*. In it, the viewer would see the Mike Wallace of 150 years past pursuing a government customs agent or contractor who's running away from the camera, all the while shouting, "So how did you wind up putting that lighthouse on the wrong island?"

Somebody goofed badly when the government sent a contractor out in 1857 with instructions to put a lighthouse next to the old fur trading center at LaPointe. The village on the west side of Madeline Island was at the center of the Apostles, and then was the chief port of western Lake Superior.

The government wanted it on Long Island, which was south of Madeline Island, on the route vessels took to get to LaPointe. Instead, the contractor put it on Michigan Island, seventeen miles to the northeast.

The government told the contractor to build another light on Long Island, or he wouldn't get paid. The government used the lighthouse on Michigan Island for a year, and then darkened it until 1869, when it decided it wanted to use the mistakenly built lighthouse after all. Eventually, officials concluded the tower was not right for the conditions at Michigan Island, and erected a taller one in 1929.

If Michigan Island is a monument to colossal goofs, there is redemption in the beauty of the light station's buildings and in at least one harrowing story involving a lighthouse keeper in the 1890s.

Visitors can reach the light station by traveling to a beach on the southwestern corner of the three-and-a-half-mile-long island, and walking up steps leading to the top of a 110-foot bluff. At the top, in a clearing in the midst of a forest, they will see an older (and non-functioning) fifty-four-foot brick and masonry tower with quarters attached.

They'll also see a 112-foot steel tower erected in 1929, and a newer quarters building. Those going to the top of the taller tower will see an optic light, with a plastic and acrylic lens, installed in 1975. If they want to see the original Fresnel lens used at Michigan Island, that's at the Visitor Center of the Apostle Islands National Lakeshore in Bayfield.

In spite of the loveliness of the place, Michigan is not among the two light stations in the Apostles included in stops in regular summertime boat trips offered by the Apostle Islands Cruise Service.

"Ones who come to Michigan really want to come," said Gene Wilkins, a retired physical therapist and petroleum geologist who lives in Texas, and a volunteer at Michigan Island in the summer season. When interviewed on Michigan Island, Wilkins was living in the newer quarters, which were completed in 1928. "Those island stations where the cruise boats go by really get a lot of visitation."

Actually, there always have been some visitors, including the ones who originally mistakenly built the lighthouse on Michigan Island.

The tale begins right after the opening of the first of the Soo Canals in 1855, when settlement and commerce into Lake Superior were expanding sharply. The government decided it was time for a lighthouse leading to LaPointe.

So, in 1857, a contractor set out for the Apostle Islands, to build the lighthouse. But in that time before instantaneous communications, the contractor apparently went to the only representative of the federal government in the area, the collector of customs. Depending on who is telling the story, either the collector mistakenly directed the contractor to Michigan Island, or local shippers talked him into building it there.

Bob Mackreth, historian for the Apostle Islands National Lakeshore, said a crew came out knowing it had to build a lighthouse, but didn't exactly know where to put it. "From what we can best reconstruct, they went to the only representative of the federal government who was out here, the collector of customs at LaPointe."

Into this came the contractor, who said, "We're here to build your lighthouse," Mackreth said.

The collector said he didn't know anything about a lighthouse, Mackreth said wryly, continuing his reconstruction of events.

The first Michigan Island lighthouse was built in 1857, darkened in 1853, relit in 1869 and replaced in 1929.

"They said, 'Well, where do you want it? We gotta build a light-house.' He said, 'Well, guess on Michigan Island would probably be the best place."

The historian chuckled. "So the crew went out. They did take much effort hauling material up the cliff. Built a fine little lighthouse on Michigan Island. There was only one problem. It wasn't where it was supposed to go. The lighthouse was supposed to go much closer to the actual port of LaPointe."

The contractor made a report to the Lighthouse Board office in Detroit on the construction of the lighthouse, and was told he wouldn't get anything until he built a station at his own expense, in the right spot, at LaPointe. The contractor built the second lighthouse the next year, and Michigan Island wasn't used.

In 1863, one of the contractors, J.B. Smith, sent a somewhat confusing letter to Lighthouse Board Chairman Rear Admiral W.B. Shubrick appealing for more money and giving his side of the story.

"(We) had a boat loaded with the material and implements for the construction of the works and a crew of thirty-eight men and laborers waiting to go to work. To have received definite instructions from Washington would have occasioned the ruinous delay of nearly if not quite two months," Smith wrote.

"I don't think we'll ever know for sure what transpired," Mackreth said.

Whatever the truth is, about eight years after the construction of the lighthouse at Michigan Island, the government decided it wanted to use it after all. But it wasn't high enough, and the government put another one in service in 1929. That second tower had been on the Delaware River in Pennsylvania near Philadelphia, and was dismantled and shipped to Michigan Island.

The story of the two lighthouses is evident to visitors to Michigan Island. But there is one story that may not be discovered by a visitor, that of the harrowing ride of Robert Carlson and his brother.

When winter came and ice covered the lake, the shipping season ended, and the lighthouses shut down until spring. Usually, keepers brought their families to the shore to spend the winter. But one winter in the mid-1890s, Michigan Island Keeper Robert Carlson and his wife, Anna Maria, decided they would spend those cold months on the island.

Anna Maria, a Swedish immigrant who lived in Chicago before she married Robert, another Swedish immigrant who had worked as a commercial fisherman, later described herself as totally intimidated by the experience of living at the light.

"She said when the men would go out during the day, she would lock the door behind, even though she knew there was no one else around," said Mackreth.

Separate photos show Robert and Anna Carlson and their children. The children, shown a few years after their father almost floated away on an ice floe, are Cecelia; and right and center, twins Robert and Carl. Photo of Robert was taken circa 1909-1913, while Anna's photo was taken in 1890.

In an account given to reporter Stella Champney of the *Detroit News* in 1931, Anna Maria described a frightful incident she said occurred when their girl was two and her twin boys were nine months old. From the known birthdays of the twins – May 25, 1894 – Mackreth speculates it may have occurred in February 1895.

One morning, the Carlson brothers went ice fishing. They didn't return by supper time or by bedtime. Anna Maria stayed up all night worrying.

"Morning found me on the verge of hysteria. But there was serious work to be done. I had to milk the cow because of the children," Anna Maria said in the account she gave to *The Detroit News*.

She hadn't personally milked the cow, but had watched her husband do it. So she went into the cow's stall, only to be chased out. Then she used an ax to chop a hole into the side of the stall, reached in, and got the milk she needed for her children.

Although she knew there was provision for her children, the fate of her husband and her brother-in-law remained a mystery.

"On the third day I could stand the house no longer. Leaving the little girl with the twins, I put on a hat and coat and went down the shore. You don't know what the Michigan Island shore is in winter. Unbroken trails through the woods, ice hummocks barring the way, deep gulches of snow into which I stumbled, the bitter, cutting wind from the lake lashing my face; and above all the sight of that white expanse which was holding my husband from me."

What she couldn't know was that the ice floe they were fishing on had broken away, and now was floating away.

If the floe continued to float to the northeast, those on it would certainly die when it broke apart. Instead, it floated to Madeline Island, four miles to the west, where the brothers hopped with difficulty onto other floes, and then to the shore. There, the Carlson brothers broke into an old fisherman's shanty. Famished and cold, they found some flour, boiled it, and regained their strength by eating the resulting gruel.

Next, they found a leaky old boat, which they repaired, using oakum and pitch they'd also found. With difficulty, they maneuvered the boat back across the lake, floating when they broke through and pushing it when they were on ice.

Meanwhile, Anna Maria had returned to her house after that walk on the shore on the third day. She fell to the floor and screamed until she was exhausted. "You know how it is with us women," she said. "Sometimes, when we think we can't endure any longer, it does us good to let go, like that. I think if I had not screamed I would have lost my mind."

Anna Maria was in the kitchen the next afternoon when she heard the voice of her husband.

"'I'm all right, Anna,' he called to me. 'Don't be afraid.'"

"The next moment I was in his arms, sobbing and laughing in real hysterics," she said.

Considering what almost happened to Robert Carlson and his brother, it would be reasonable to conclude that somebody was being foolishly frugal in deciding to spend the winter on Michigan Island. In fact, said Mackreth, Anna Maria's account made it clear the family stayed on the island over the winter to avoid having to take their three young children off the island at the end of the season.

"Having been out on the lake in late autumn myself, I can appreciate her concerns," said Mackreth.

"When I look at the building of Michigan Island, I think of the horrendous mix-up in putting the lighthouse in the wrong place," Mackreth said. But then, "I look at the buildings and I see how beautiful they are." Finally, he thinks of what happened the winter the Carlson brothers went ice fishing, and what occurred before no longer matters.

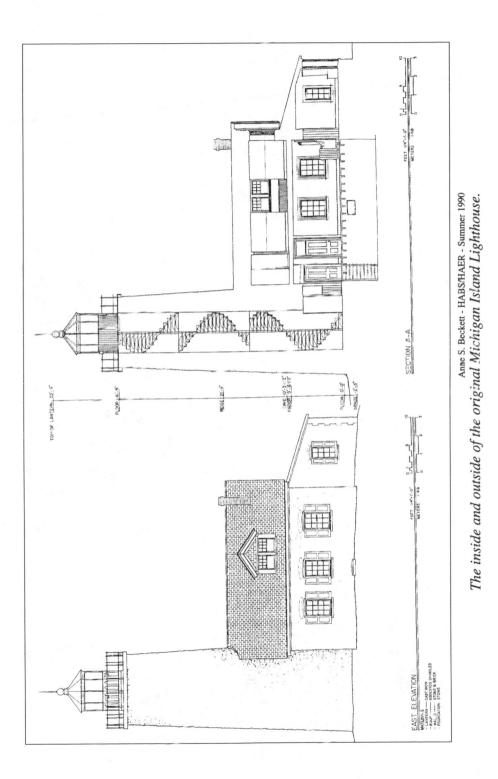

Anne S. Beckett - HABS/HAER - Summer 1990

The inside and outside of the original Michigan Island Lighthouse.

The second Michigan Island light tower started its career at Schooner's Ledge on the Delaware River near Philadelphia, before it was erected and lit in 1929.

Chapter Three
Long Island:
The Overlooked Lights

On his first visit to the light station on Long Island, Jim Nepstad had an experience that illustrates the impression many have about the station's historic navigational aids.

"I had kind of been told that this particular light is not quite as historic as some of the other lights in the lakeshore," said Nepstad, management assistant for the Apostle Islands National Lakeshore.

"I went with low expectations and walked away really pleased with it," said Nepstad, who made his first visit to the light station in September 1999, not long after he came to the Apostle Islands. "The location . . . is probably one of the nicest physical locations for a lighthouse within the lakeshore. It's just right off of a beautiful sandy beach."

Also called the LaPointe Light Station, the station on Long Island is often the last considered and last visited of the Apostle Islands National Lakeshore lighthouses. One popular lighthouse book, for example, listed the Apostle Islands light stations at Devils, Sand, Outer, Raspberry and Michigan islands as attractions on the southern shore of Lake Superior, but left off the one at Long Island.

Periodic cruises take tourists in a sweep past the other five light stations, but bypass Long Island. Dave Strzok, who operates the Apostle Islands Cruise Service, said Long Island is too far out of the way to be part of the tour. In addition, shallow water extending into the lake prevents cruise boats from coming close enough for a good view, while trees make it hard to see the towers.

If it appears there's a conspiracy to diminish the importance of the navigational aids on Long Island, that's nothing new. Seemingly, that plot began even before there was a lighthouse on that narrow sand spit.

By a foul-up detailed in the previous chapter, a contractor built a lighthouse seventeen miles to the northeast, on Michigan Island, instead of Long Island, where the government wanted it. Hence, what should have been the first lighthouse in the Apostle Islands was actually the second.

A more recent omission also worked to make the buildings and two light towers of the Long Island Light Station the most overlooked of the six stations of the Apostle Islands National Lakeshore.

"Long Island was not added to the National Lakeshore until considerably after the rest of the islands," said Bob Mackreth, historian at the National Lakeshore. While the lakeshore was created in 1970, Long Island wasn't part of the lakeshore until the middle of the 1980s.

"We're not as far along in the process of restoring and stabilizing the lights as we are with the rest of them," Mackreth said. "The buildings have received basic stabilization. They have not received quite the same amount of work that the others have yet. We'll eventually rectify that situation, but of course it takes time."

As if that's not enough, Long Island isn't even an island, but a continuous chunk of sand extending northwest from the south shore of Lake Superior. A map published in 1964 showed a narrow island separated from a sand spit, extending to the south shore. The island reconnected to the mainland in the 1975 storm that sank the freighter *Edmund Fitzgerald*, killing twenty-nine and inspiring Gordon Lightfoot's ballad "The Wreck of the Edmund Fitzgerald."

"Geologists tell us that Long Island has joined and split from the mainland many times over the centuries," Mackreth said.

Visitors to the island will learn details of the construction of the light station there, including the mistake that deprived Long Island of the "First Lighthouse in the Apostle Islands" status, and how there came to be two light towers on that island.

Neither of the two existing towers is the original one. That was built in 1858 by the same contractor who mistakenly erected the lighthouse on Michigan Island in 1857. The federal government had told him to erect a light in the right place, or forfeit any chance of payment. That contractor hastily built a wooden tower on a squared timber foundation, about a quarter mile east of the western end of Long Island.

In that location, the light was on the south end of a one-and-a-mile-wide channel. On the north end of that channel was Madeline Island, and the village of LaPointe.

The lighthouse didn't go on Madeline Island because of the route ships took to LaPointe. They came from the east, on the southern side of Madeline Island. LaPointe is in a harbor on the west side of Madeline.

"If you put the light originally at the mouth of the LaPointe Harbor, they'd practically be on top of it before they got there," Mackreth said. "The light would essentially be hidden from the sea lanes by the corner of Madeline Island, Grant's Point."

For most of the rest of the 1800s, the lighthouse and its keeper did their part in saving lives of mariners who passed nearby. But there was nothing the keeper could do to save the lives of the nine crew members of the schooner barge *Lucerne* when it grounded just off Long Island in a November gale in 1886.

The Chequamegon Point Light, at the western end of Long Island, was lit in 1897. Its beacon is now on a nearby modern cylindrical tower.

The original LaPointe Light tower was erected in 1858 and replaced in 1897.

What the keeper saw after the grounding still provides good material for Apostle Islands storytellers.

"When he looked out, he saw the rigging of the ship sticking up above the water with three sailors frozen to the masts," Mackreth told an audience at the 1998 Apostle Islands Lighthouse Celebration. Six others on the *Lucerne* drowned. Divers still can see today the remains of the schooner, off Long Island.

More changes came in the 1890s, beginning with the installation of a fog signal east of the first lighthouse. The station's logbook records that on October 11, 1897, two lights a mile apart from each other went into service, replacing the original 1858 light. To the east, workers erected a sixty-nine-foot cylindrical tower, next to the fog signal. It is today called the LaPointe Light. On the island's far northwestern end, at Chequamegon Point, they put up a forty-two-foot tower, which held the 4th Order Fresnel lens that was in the original building.

The original old clapboard building was renovated in the years that followed, used as a dwelling and eventually abandoned. Today the building located about 1,000 feet west of the LaPointe tower is in ruins.

"It's not marked or signed, but it's easy enough to find, and people are certainly welcome to visit it. You do need to use care, though, since it is a ruin," Mackreth said. "What's interesting is that when it was built, it was close to the water, but the way the shoreline has shifted, it is well inland."

By the time the 1890s arrived, the importance of LaPointe had declined, while the important new city of Ashland emerged, about twelve miles south of Long Island in Chequamegon Bay. Ashland became a major Great Lakes port in the late 1800s and early 1900s.

"The point of putting the light in at Chequamegon Point, the very tip, was not so much to guide ships to LaPointe now, but to give them an idea of where the end of Long Island was, that they'd have to swing around in order to get to Ashland," Mackreth said. "We're looking at lighthouses that are really serving entirely separate functions. The original point of the Long Island Light was to guide ships to LaPointe. By the turn of the century, they were much more interested in providing beacons that would guide ships into Ashland Harbor."

With two lights and more fog signals, the keeper of the light station on Long Island found himself needing extra help. Extra staff people hired to deal with the new tower cramped the original clapboard keepers' quarters at the light station. This problem was solved when that house was placed on top of a new brick first floor.

The twentieth century brought additional changes. In 1924, a radio beacon was installed. To provide power for the beacon and the quarters, generators were brought in. Then in 1938, the Works Progress Administration built a new triplex quarters near the LaPointe Light. Both lights were fully automated in 1964.

More change came in 1987 when a helicopter picked up the Chequamegon Point tower and moved it back from the eroding shore-line. Meanwhile the old Chequamegon Point Light went dark, when its beacon was moved to a practical but less interesting cylindrical tower.

It's been years since keepers and their families lived at Long Island. But Lois Spangle, whose father, Alphonse L. Gustafson, was stationed there from the late 1930s to the mid-1940s, keeps alive the memory of those days.

Life on an island didn't deprive Spangle of companionship. "I would go out during the summer and bring either my friends or my cousins out there. I also had other friends out there who were children of commercial fishermen," Spangle recalled.

Those fishermen and their families lived in three shanties, near the keepers' quarters, Spangle said. "There was a lot of company for me."

An annual event for Spangle and her family was the visit of the inspectors, usually some time in July.

"They would inspect the dwelling, the signal house and everything connected with the lighthouse there. The men would have to meet them down at the dock, and they would have to have their uniforms on," Spangle said. "None of them knew when they were coming, but through the grapevine, they would kind of get an idea."

"All of the dustpans and the oil cans and everything had to be polished, and the floors were always painted," Spangle said. "Everything had to be painted, clean. Very, very clean. And then they would go into the lighthouse tower and check that out, to see if there is any imperfection on the light itself," Spangle said.

Sometime later, a letter would come, telling the results of the inspection. "That would give them their notice of their next annual paycheck increases," she said with a laugh. "They never failed in anything."

Spangle's memories of the light station continued even after she was married in 1945. Her first child had a first birthday celebration on the island in 1948. In later years, Spangle and her husband, Ernie, would take a fifteen-foot boat out to the island and pitch a tent there.

On trips to the island in the late 1940s and early 1950s, the Spangles would have encountered Robert E. Parker, Sr., a Coast Guardsman who served on Long Island from April 1946 to the middle of the summer of 1952.

"There was a concrete walk that ran from the fog signal, all the way down to the Chequamegon Point Light," Parker wrote, in a letter to the author. "We were told by the keeper that we should never travel this walk during a rain storm, when there was a lot of lightning." Apparently, the blocks were reinforced with steel, which acted as a lightning rod.

"The real surprising thing about this walk was that this whole mile of cement blocks (was) shipped all of the way up here from Staten Island, N.Y., which was the supply depot for all lighthouse supplies at one time. There was a date on each of the blocks and if my memory is correct, the date was 1903 with the letters USLHE, signifying United States Lighthouse Establishment," Parker wrote.

In the 1990s, he returned to Long Island, but couldn't find the walkway. "It's there somewhere, but must be covered over with drifted sand, I guess," he wrote.

"There was the finest swimming beach that a person could find, out on the island. There were lots of wild blueberries and raspberries. Good fishing, not only in Lake Superior, but in the adjoining Chequamegon Bay water. At one time, there were many rabbits on the island, but when a family of red foxes decided to make the island their home, the rabbits soon disappeared."

For Spangle and for Parker, such pleasures of life on Long Island are old news. Others, such as Nepstad, didn't know all that awaited them, until they made a visit to this out-of-the-way place.

Nepstad attributes his turnaround at least in part to the mystique of lighthouses. "Even when you climb up to the top of a tower that might not be quite as old as other towers that you've been in, there's just something magical about being up in a lighthouse tower and looking out over Lake Superior."

Apostle Islands National Lakeshore
The LaPointe Light on Long Island was lit in 1897.

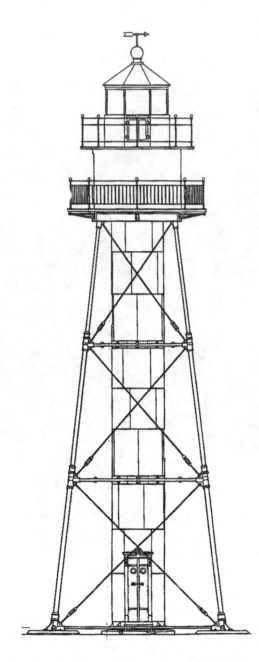

Krzysztof Koszewski - HABS/HAER - Summer 1991
The LaPointe Light Station Tower.

Chapter Four
Raspberry Island:
The Storybook Light

Annie is only the creation of a writer of a dramatic musical play. Nonetheless, the tale of this fictitious lighthouse keeper's daughter catches the spirit of the real Raspberry Island Light Station, a storybook place in the Apostle Islands.

In Warren Nelson's *Keeper of the Light*, Annie describes what happened when she was nine, and traveled with her mother from the family farm in Iowa to rejoin her father, the newly named Raspberry Island keeper.

The story of Annie, based on the accounts of real-life keepers' families, inspires audiences each summer when they see it performed at the Lake Superior Big Top Chautauqua, south of Bayfield. Those who take the regular summertime excursion boats from Bayfield to the Raspberry Island Light may be similarly inspired, and sense what Annie sensed, as she approached the island the first time.

"The assistant motored us out, and father was yelling over the racket of the engine about garden plots and fruit trees and my room that had a window that looked out over the lake," Annie tells the audience in one of several vignettes of the production about Apostle Islands lighthouses.

"There just up ahead, was our very first look at the beautiful Raspberry Island Light. Oh. 'Which window is mine?' I yelled. 'Are there whales and mermaids?'"

There are no stories of whales and mermaids on Raspberry Island, a mile-long, hourglass-shaped island that got its name from the Ojibway Indians. But there are tales just as interesting about this island that arise from more than 135 years' service as a sentinel for mariners.

Lit in the same month as the Union victory at Gettysburg, the Raspberry Island Lighthouse was the third light station constructed in the Apostle Islands, and the first on the western end of the archipelago. The lighthouse about one and one-half miles from the mainland gained a special importance as waterborne trade picked up between two port areas on the south shore of western Lake Superior. On the western end of Lake Superior was Duluth. About eighty miles to the east, in a splendid harbor protected by the Apostle Islands, were the port towns of Bayfield and Ashland.

The mariners traveling between those ports found comfort in the 5th Order Fresnel lens at Raspberry Island after it went into service on July 20, 1863.

In 1881, another light was lit on the western end of the Apostles, at Sand Island. But that beacon west of the Raspberry Island Light didn't diminish the importance of the one at Raspberry. In 1887, an official of a steamer that traversed waters near the light wrote a letter to the secretary of the treasury attesting to its value. In that letter, J.C. Thompson, master of the steamer *Horace A. Tuttle*, called the light at Raspberry Island the most important one between Duluth, Bayfield and Ashland. As readers will learn, the circumstances behind that letter almost got a Raspberry Island keeper fired.

Change came with the start of the twentieth century. In 1902, a red brick fog signal building was added, along with a ten-inch steam whistle and a hoisting engine for a tramway.

The new steam whistle meant more people would be working at the light station. Because of this, the lighthouse was divided in 1906-1907 so the keeper and two assistants could have private quarters.

More changes came in 1928 with the installation of a twenty-three kilowatt, diesel-driven electric generator. Five years later, two diesel engines and two air compressors were installed in the fog signal building. With that, the steam whistle converted to a diaphone, or a foghorn producing a low-pitched, penetrating signal.

Then in 1947, the light was automated, ending the need for keepers on the island. Five years after that, the light was placed in a metal tower in front of the fog signal building.

Today, the 5th Order Fresnel lens of the Raspberry Island Lighthouse is in the Madeline Island Historical Museum, on Madeline Island, a two-and-a-half mile ferry ride from Bayfield. But the heart of that lighthouse remains on Raspberry Island.

Today, as one of two Apostle Island light stations accessible to regular summertime cruise boats, the light station is restored as it was in the 1920s and 1930s, complete with a garden plot to the rear of the light station.

"According to letters and journals written during the days of manned light stations, lightkeepers' families competed with each other for productive and beautiful gardens," Dave Strzok, owner of the Apostle Islands Cruise Service, wrote in his book, *The Visitor's Guide to the Apostle Islands National Lakeshore*.

"The Raspberry Lighthouse flower gardens were acknowledged as being the most beautiful as they framed the large white duplex," Strzok wrote.

But there was much more to Raspberry Island than pretty flowers and plants.

Francis Jacker, Raspberry Island Lighthouse keeper from 1885 to 1892, knew the island for an unfortunate experience that convinced his superiors to grant his request for extra help.

Jacker's grief was that a tightfisted Lighthouse Service would not hear his pleas for reinstatement of an assistant keeper.

The light at Raspberry Island first went on in 1863, right after the Union victory at Gettysburg.

"In case of an emergency, no assistance is available on the island, and the proper surveillance of the revolving apparatus during the long nights of the fall when frequent windings are required, is exhausting," he wrote in his log.

Jacker's prayers were answered, but not the way he would have preferred. On the morning of September 13, 1887, a westerly gale developed, which endangered the station's sailboat, which had been anchored near the dock on the southwest tip of the island.

"Jumping out of bed, I hurried to move it to a place of safety at the eastern extremity of the island – the dilapidated condition of the ways rendering it impossible, for the moment, to have it hauled up to the boat house."

But in the dark, Jacker sailed by the landing point. In the storm, he was forced to sail southeast. "I could do nothing but to sail, under reefed canvas, with the current of the wind and waves, thus drifting over to Oak Island."

The storm continued for three days, as Jacker remained stranded on an island two miles from his own. When the weather finally cleared, the boat was wrecked, making it impossible for him to use it for a return trip. He might never have returned had it not been for a passing Indian, who noticed his distress signal and rescued him.

"I had spent nearly three days on the desolated island, without food, without fire and being but scantily dressed," he wrote in his log.

What made Jacker's misfortunes particularly bad was this fact: he was alone on the island, because his family wasn't with him at the lighthouse. Without the assistant he requested, there was no one to light the light.

"In consequence of the above occurrence, the light of this station was not extinguished in the morning of the 13th, and not exhibited the night following. It was relighted, however, in the night of the 14th and 15th by my family who happened to come for a visit, but owing to their inability to get the revolving machinery into motion, the apparatus did not revolve," said the entry in Jacker's log.

While Jacker had escaped with his life, a question remained whether he would escape with his job. For the light had gone out, which was an offense worthy of a reprimand or a dismissal. Indeed, word of the extinguished light got to the U.S. secretary of the treasury. On September 22, 1887, J.C. Thompson, master of the steamer *Horace A. Tuttle,* wrote a letter to the treasury secretary informing him that the Raspberry Island Light was darkened when he had passed by a few days before. Wanting to know why this happened, Thompson said Raspberry Island was "important, because it is the leading light between Duluth, Bayfield and Ashland."

Visitors on a stop at the Raspberry Island Lighthouse head from the dock up the stairway to the station. The Raspberry Island Lighthouse is one of the two Apostle Islands light stations that are visited in the summertime by regular cruises. The Sand Island Lighthouse is the other one.

When the district inspector demanded an explanation, Jacker responded with the story of how he was blown onto Oak Island. By the end of the year, Francis Jacker's brother, Edward Jacker, received the appointment as assistant keeper of the Raspberry Island Lighthouse.

Thirty-five years passed, and a man whose name today is well known around the Apostles came to work at the Raspberry Island Light. But it's not because of skill or dedication that Herbert "Toots" Winfield today has that local renown. It is rather for Winfield's failures that he is now famous, seven decades after his service ended at Raspberry Island.

The man who made Toots known is Matt Welter. From 1992 to 1998, those coming to Raspberry Island knew Welter as Toots, who was an assistant keeper of that island's lighthouse in the 1920s. Welter dressed, acted and talked as the free-living "Toots," to give visitors a taste of life at his lighthouse in an earlier time.

Welter has a theory about why the bachelor Winfield never moved up to keeper. "It's never really indicated, but I have a feeling why he didn't. I think he was comfortable," he said.

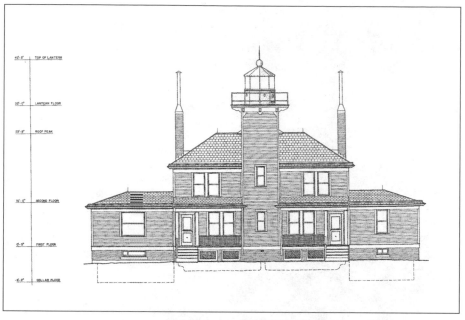

Lisa Monning - HABS/HAER - Summer 1989
The Raspberry Island Lighthouse.

One unusual thing Welter notes about Toots is what was written in logs about the company he brought to the island. Those logs would note the names of the friends and relatives of the other keepers who visited. "But when Toots would have people there, it would always say in the log book something like 'The assistant had a group of young people out at the lighthouse, and they tented out on the lawn last night and they made quite a ruckus,'" Welter said.

"The reason why he was fired was that he was found drunk on duty, in '31." Welter said. "Toots Winfield went around in 1930 to a bunch of speakeasies with a bunch of lighthouse keepers and got the whole town mad at him because they weren't really lighthouse keepers, they were prohibition officers in disguise. So he pretty much ostracized himself from the town."

However, Welter said, it does tell the story that Winfield probably was hitting all the speakeasies in town when he was on shore.

"One of the stories I would tell people is 'We don't have to cut firewood here at the lighthouse, because, we can just go down to the beach and gather all the logs that come by, 'cause those Canadian boats will come down to the mills there in Ashland, and they'll bring a big raft of logs, and sometimes they'll lose a few. And they float up to our place and once they land on the island they're part of the keeper's reserve,'" said Welter, speaking in the voice of Toots.

"Every time I find 'em I go down and knock on 'em, 'cause if they sound hollow, it could mean whisky. Then I'd say, being a federal officer, I'd have to destroy all of that. A little at a time, but I'd have to destroy it all."

Though Toots Winfield was based on a real character, much of what Welter had him saying was necessarily based on his imagination. The encounters Roberta Rippel and her husband, Tony, have had with the Raspberry Island Lighthouse are more real, even though they too spark the imagination.

Tony Rippel runs a charter fishing boat out of Bayfield called, appropriately, Roberta's Sport Fishing & Scuba Diving. Both were owners of the Apostle Islands Outfitters in Bayfield before they sold it in 1991 to Larry and Julie MacDonald. (Larry is Bayfield's mayor.) Roberta still works at Apostle Islands Outfitters, while her husband operates the charter fishing boat. The couple and their adult son live on County Highway K, about a mile from the lake, and about two miles from the light.

Roberta speaks lovingly of the breathtaking views they have.

"You can see it flashing at night, and once in a while – it depends – somebody may have lights on out there and we can see the lights," she said. "You see the sun in the morning shining on the island. Then in the day it moves across. Then come nighttime, it just shines on it so pretty," she said, "It looks like the lighthouse is on fire, the sun hitting the windows."

Sometimes Rippel and her husband see a ship going between the land and the island.

"They're magical," she said of lighthouses. "They're just neat."

Like others who have encountered Raspberry Island, Rippel might echo the words of Annie's mother in *Keeper of the Light,* "Back there's the mainland, out there's the dreamland, and my home is here in between, on an island."

Chapter Five
Outer Island:
A Place of Remoteness
and Beauty

The closest anyone can get to the edge of the world without leaving Wisconsin may be at the northeastern edge of the Apostles, on Outer Island.

More than thirty miles from Bayfield, this was a lonely place for the keepers and families who worked at the lighthouse on the island's northern end after it went into service in 1874.

"When you talk about romance and loneliness, it's kind of hard to beat the Outer Island station for its beauty and its setting," said Bob Mackreth, historian for the Apostle Islands National Lakeshore. In a talk at the 1998 Apostle Islands Lighthouse Celebration, Mackreth spoke of the loneliness and beauty of the island, and of the world-class sunsets available for viewing for the visitor. "To my mind, it's strictly one of the most aesthetically appealing of the Apostle Islands lighthouses."

Yet that setting means only a few visitors to the Apostles get a close look at the Outer Island Lighthouse. "It's perhaps the least-visited lighthouse of all the Apostle Islands, but when people go there, I know they are impressed by its beauty," said Bob Wiinamaki, a former cruise boat captain in the Apostles.

Those who come to the island climb a stairway leading up a forty-foot red-clay bluff. On top of the bluff, another climb awaits to the top of the ninety-foot tower, by way of a cast-iron spiral staircase leading to a watchroom.

With hooded arched windows and decorated brackets supporting the watchroom walkway, the whitewashed brick lighthouse tower is clearly influenced by the Italianate architectural style of the 1860s and 1870s. At the bottom of the tower, a wooden passageway leads to the three-story red brick keeper's quarters.

What the visitor won't see is a 3rd Order Fresnel lens, with a central band of six glass prism bull's-eye panels. In the late 1930s, the light was electrified, allowing automatic operation in the winter, when keepers weren't present. The Fresnel lens was removed in 1961, when the station was fully automated.

The location of the lens today is anybody's guess.

"I did my lighthouse program the other night and one of the things I said was, 'Anybody know where the Outer Island light is?'" Mackreth said. When nobody responded, he said, "I'll keep asking."

In a nearby building, visitors can see a fog signal run by air compressors and diesel engines, installed in 1925. That replaced a locomotive whistle, with a coal-fired boiler used to build up steam pressure.

"The fog signal at Outer Island is in the best condition of any of the fog signals here in the Apostles," Mackreth said. "None of the historic fog signals are operational. This is the one that's closest to its original condition. Who knows? Perhaps some day they might be able to restore it."

As much as the buildings attract the history and lighthouse enthusiast, there are simpler pleasures awaiting, such as the view from the top of the light tower.

When John Irvine looked out from the Outer Island Light Station on September 2, 1905, he wasn't thinking about the pleasant view.

Irvine, who was keeper at Outer Island for more than ten years starting in March 1898, began his entries in the station's log book for September 2, 1905 the same way he almost always did. To preserve the flavor of the entries, it is printed almost exactly as written, with few corrections of grammar and spelling.

"2 - Cleaning, Triming Lamps and Lens. Tending Signal."

The monotony ended with the next sentence.

"A Terable gale blowing from the NE, the Bigest Sea that I have seen since I have been at the station which is eight years. About 2:30 PM, sighted a Schooner at anchor about two miles NE of Station. About 4 PM seen [a] small boat leaving Schooner. I, the Keeper, huried down the beach with a white flag in my hand, and a piece of rope to render what assistance I could. I helped to pull five men ashore, pretty well escausted. Five were drowned. The crew consisted [of] Captain Charles Smart and nine of a crew. The Captain, Mate, and three Seamen were saved. Four seamen, and the cook who was colored, was drowned.

"Sunday 3- Cleaning, triming Lamps and Lens. Doing what we could for the comfort of the Captain and his four men who was saved last night. They are all much improved today after a good nights rest and sleep. Weather moderating.

"4- Cleaning, triming Lamps and Lens and other necessary work. Tending to the resceud men. They were all able to go along the beach looking for the bodies of those that perished. None were found. They all got back to the station by Noon. While at dinner, the Steamer "Venezuela" came in sight looking for her consort, which was the "Pretoria," which she could plainly see as it looks like too thirds of her

The Outer Island Light Station was first illuminated in 1874.

The appearance of the Outer Island Light Station has changed little since this photo was taken around 1900.

Spars is above water. We signaled the Steamer. She sent a boat ashore at 2 PM, and took the men off. The sea was pretty well run down so that they did not have any trouble in landing here. The "Pretoria" hailed from Duluth. She belonged to Captain James Davidson of Bay City, Mich. She was loaded with iron ore from Aloucies Bay [bound] for South Chicago. I ecpect She will be a Total Wreck as her decks is all coming ashore."

The entries describe one of two wrecks that occurred the same day in the Apostles in a historic Lake Superior storm.

Towed by the tug *Venezuela,* the schooner barge *Pretoria* went down after the towline between the two vessels snapped, just north of Outer Island. During the same storm, the steamship *Sevona* broke apart when it struck a shoal on the western end of the Apostles, near the Sand Island Lighthouse, sending seven to their deaths.

It's the kind of story that excites lovers of lighthouse stories. But it was in fact a horrendous break from the routine of life at the Outer Island Lighthouse. Indeed, the log did report the wedding in Bayfield on August 23 of Irvine's son and first assistant, Thomas E. Irvine. It also reported how the younger Irvine came back on September 5 with his young wife and Robert Irvine, "a Brother of the Keeper, who had not seen each other for 28 years."

That excitement aside, much of the logbook that Irvine kept is filled with reports of his daily cleaning and trimming the lamps and lenses, along with other routine matters.

Gene Wilkins knows well how routine the entries could be. A retiree from Texas, he's served for several years as a summertime volunteer at light stations in the Apostles.

In off-seasons, he painstakingly made his way through about 1,300 pages of microfilmed Outer Island logbooks from 1874 to 1947, transcribing them onto computer disks. His efforts to copy the log, word for word and misspelling for misspelling, only making minor changes and comments when absolutely necessary, are reflected in the excerpts from the log printed here.

"It was interesting to see the different personalities that shined through in different keepers as they would make entry into the log," Wilkins said. From his work, Wilkins notes the interaction that occurred between the keepers and the fishermen on the south end of the island.

The logbook also reveals that most years from 1874 to 1880 there were people at the Outer Island Lighthouse all year long. This is in spite of the fact that winter ice brought the shutdown of Lake Superior light stations from December through the start of spring.

The year-round nature adds to the drama of some of the log entries in the early years at the station. As before, it is the way the keeper wrote it, with misspellings and grammatical errors left in.

"1876

"February 7 - Walked to other side of the island called Sand Point. From the observation it appears all frozen between Hemlock, Presquele and this Island. Ice water between Michigan and this. In coming home undertook to come on southeast side thus making the crook of the Island, but found water close to shore about 2 miles up. Was forced to walk back and take the NW side again. Left at 1 PM arrived home 6 1/2 PM. Walked about 20 miles. The smooth ice is only about 6" thick. Don't think it safe to try and go to Bayfield yet.

"April 10 .. At 4 AM the 3rd Assistant arrives, a boy, weighs 8 1/2 lbs. troy weight. This is an important event, at least to me. Mother and Babe are doing well.

"1879

"Thursday (December) 25- SW, light, clear. Sunshine this forenoon. Ther. 13 below at 7 AM; 20 at 10 AM; moderated to 18 by 9 PM. Wind fresh, NW, tonight. Lake full of drifting ice all day. The children enjoyed their first Christmas Tree very much.

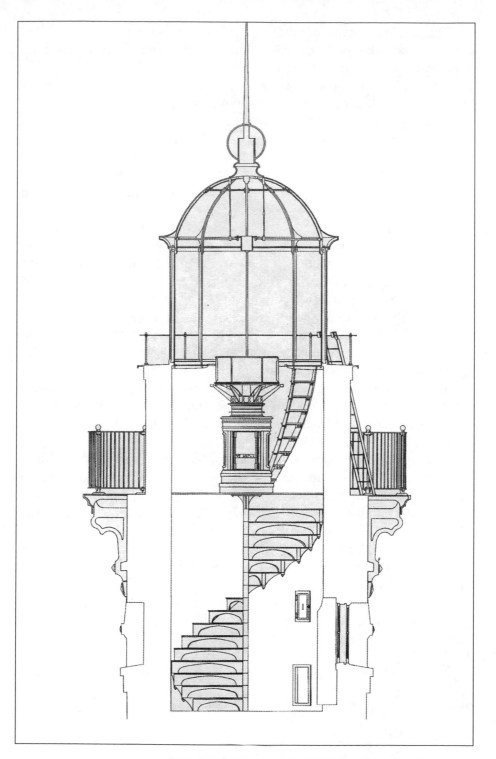

Kenneth W. Martin - HABS/HAER - Summer 1990
The Outer Island Light Station tower.

"1880

"Tuesday (January) 13- SE, light, cloudy. 4 below to 20 above. The Second Assistant and I went half way across to the Cat (Island) [and] examining the ice find it very rough all the way. On coming close to shore on our way back found the ice had moved off from 20 to 40 feet. By running back a piece we managed to get ashore by jumping from cake to cake of ice, and none too soon.

"Saturday (October) 16-[..] By 2 o'clock it blew a Hurricane accompanied by heavy rain. It blew the hardest from 3:30 AM to 12 midnight tearing up trees, snapping off large hemlock and birch at the trunk as if but saplings. Between here and the landing, also back of the clearing, more than half of the trees are blown down. The cap on top of the chimney blowed off. Some of the planks off the sidewalk were thrown 20 feet away. The Tower swayed like the top of a tree; and the Lens, well, it is a wonder to me that a piece of it is left. It was sublime and grand in its fury."

Although the storms make life rough for the keepers and their families, Wilkins said, "It wasn't a hard job, like say the stone masons or quarry miners."

Whether the keepers' lives were hard or easy, their presence helped to ease the mind of people like Wiinamaki. He sees a source of comfort for his father, in the nearly fifty years the elder Wiinamaki sailed on the Great Lakes.

"It's very close to me because I know they have been a part of my family, my father's life, all his life on the Great Lakes," Wiinamaki said.

Robert E. Parker Sr. has an even closer connection to Outer Island. The Hermantown, Minn., resident was in the Coast Guard from 1941 to 1961, and officer in charge of the Outer Island Station in 1953.

"All these lights were the same at the time. They had their own generators and battery banks for electricity and they had their own motor launch for running into town for supplies and mail," he said. Running eight to nine miles an hour, it took about three and one-half hours to get into Bayfield, he said.

"They get some pretty good storms on Lake Superior, especially in the fall," said Parker, who was one of four men stationed at Outer Island.

In the late 1940s, Parker's brother, Walter, was involved in the recovery of an important artifact of Outer Island, while he was in charge of the Coast Guard moorings in Bayfield. On a visit to Outer Island, he got into a conversation with two men stationed there, who had been swimming on the beach near the dock.

"I found a bell. There's a bell at the bottom of the lake," one of them told Walter Parker. "They dove down and they tried to move it. But it (was) attached to a piece of timber." Eventually, the bell was raised to the top of the water.

It was the bell from the Pretoria, above the water for the first time since Sept. 2, 1905. So Lake Superior could claim the Pretoria, but couldn't keep all of it. Appropriately, those who helped bring it up were successors of John Irvine, the Outer Island keeper who was present when the vessel went down.

Chapter Six
Sand Island:
Memories of Two Shipwrecks
and a Brownstone Beauty

From the top of the Sand Island Lighthouse tower, visitors today can get a good view of the north shore of Minnesota, or the beam from the Devils Island Light Station to the northeast, on a starry night. Those in a thoughtful mood might make a life-changing decision, as they look out from the lighthouse that has provided a beacon on the western end of the Apostle Islands since 1881.

But for Sand Island Lighthouse Keeper Emmanuel Luick, a look to the northeast from that tower may have provided an awful reminder of the monumental storm of September 2, 1905.

Luick, who was keeper of the Sand Island Lighthouse from 1892 until the light automated in 1921, watched helplessly through binoculars as the steamer *Sevona* broke apart on the Sand Island Shoals.

Although seventeen made it to shore in two lifeboats, Capt. Donald Sutherland McDonald and six others weren't as lucky. They cast off in a makeshift lifeboat and almost made it to shore, before huge breakers tore the raft apart. Eventually, all the bodies were found on a beach on Sand Island. So, until Luick transferred from the lighthouse when it automated in 1921, he had a sharp reminder of the terror of that day in September 1905.

The wreck of the *Sevona* was hardly the only one in the Apostles, and is one of two dramatic sinkings associated with Sand Island. But around the Apostle Islands National Lakeshore, and its six historic light stations, the story of the *Sevona* is a favorite.

And so is Sand Island a favorite of people like Bob Mackreth, historian of the Apostle Islands National Lakeshore.

"No matter what time of day, there's something about it that appeals to me," Mackreth said, comparing the Sand Island Light Station to the other five light stations in the Apostles. "To me, if I had to pick one that's close to my heart, I'd definitely say Sand Island. But that's kind of like asking a parent, 'Which is your favorite kid?'"

It's not for length of years of service that people are attracted to the Sand Island Lighthouse. Lit in 1881, the ten-sided, 4th Order Fresnel Lens of the Sand Island Lighthouse gave out a fixed white light for forty years.

In that time, two principal keepers kept the light burning for passing vessels until it was replaced by an acetylene light operated by an automatic clock in 1921. Until the light was completely automated in 1933, it was maintained by the keeper of the nearby Raspberry Island Lighthouse.

Boaters and visitors for much of the time after the light station automated in 1921 got a marred view of the lighthouse's grandeur, because the light shone from a steel tower in front of the building. Today, the lighthouse looks more closely like it should, as an automated light shines from inside the forty-four-foot tower.

While illuminating, details of the light station's history are insufficient to explain its charm. Much of that charm is in the setting, on a rocky high spot on the northeastern corner of the island, with its back to trees, including a grove of virgin white pine within the lighthouse reservation, dating back to the 1700s.

But other lighthouses have good views. What sets the Sand Island Lighthouse apart is the brownstone brick on the outside, and its Norman Gothic style.

The locally-quarried brownstone gives it an appearance that would make the house fit in well in an old business district. For brownstone is abundant in the area around the Apostles. Late in the nineteenth century, quarries in the Bayfield area supplied material for row houses as far away as Chicago and New York City, and important buildings in Wisconsin, Minnesota, Iowa and other states.

The brownstone brick on the Sand Island Lighthouse appeals to Randall Peterson, an artist from Forest Lake, Minn., who makes drawings of lighthouses in the pointillism style of the French artist Georges Seurat.

Peterson was so impressed with the Sand Island Lighthouse, he decided to offer not one, but two different prints of the place for sale.

The first time Peterson saw the lighthouse he was on a boat taking pictures for what he thought would be his only drawing of Sand Island. "It was a beautiful view from the boat after the fog had lifted, looking at the lighthouse, the wild flowers surrounding it with the trees in the background," he said.

He saw the need for a second view when he took the two-mile hike from the dock at Sand Island to the lighthouse.

Although that hike to the Sand Island Lighthouse may be tough for those out-of-shape, getting on the island has been easy for Peterson and others who have come to the island in recent years. Of the six historic light stations of the Apostle Islands National Lakeshore, the lighthouses at Sand and Raspberry islands are the only ones accessible by a scheduled cruise during the summer.

"As we completed our two-mile journey, the back of (the) lighthouse stood before us," Peterson said. "As we walked the grounds, we were mesmerized by the beauty of the lighthouse and the grounds. To me the feeling was so much different from when I saw it from the boat."

The light from the Sand Island Light Station first fired the sky in 1881.

Sand Island Lighthouse Keeper Emmanuel Luick may have taken this picture, possibly of an assistant.

While the view Peterson got from the lake was two-dimensional, what he saw from the island itself was more three-dimensional. "It brought to life the lighthouse, the rich color of the brownstone, all the angles of the structure."

From that vantage point on the shore, Peterson found himself amazed that people could build such a structure on an island in Lake Superior in 1881. And he found himself wondering what it was like for the keepers and their families to live there.

Others have wondered the same thing, and had the same thoughts, even if they don't have Peterson's artistic sensitivity.

Frederick Hansen, a fisherman who lived and worked on the island until shortly before he died in 1939, visited the lighthouse and picnicked there occasionally.

"Went to Light on a picnic in morning," said a July 4, 1913, entry in the diary, which was edited and published by Hansen's grandson, Frederick H. Dahl, in 1989. "Didn't do anything - was lonesome - walked over as far as the light," said the entry for Sunday, August 24, 1913, in yet another indication of the therapeutic value of lighthouses. Another entry, on April 25, 1913, notes, "I and Louis Moe launched our boats today. Emanual (sic) Luick came out."

From such notations in a fisherman's diary, it becomes apparent that the keepers of the Sand Island Lighthouse did not share the isolation of most island lighthouses. From around the 1860s to the 1940s, it was, along with Madeline Island, one of two inhabited islands of the twenty-two Apostle Islands.

First settled by Frank Shaw, the island was the site of the Camp Stella resort in the late 1800s and early 1900s. Norwegian fishermen started settling the East Bay area around 1880. Life was difficult for the little settlement, which never grew to more than a hundred or so. In spite of this, there was a school, a post office from 1911 to 1916, a co-operative association and even a short-lived telephone company.

Into this environment came the first keeper, Charles Lederle, in 1881. He will forever be known for a single act of heroism on September 12, 1885. Lederle showed the courage of the finest lighthouse keepers when he looked out from his observation point and saw the Canadian steamer *Prussia* in flames. The boat was bound, light, from Port Arthur (now part of Thunder Bay, Ontario) to Duluth to pick up a load of grain and take it to Montreal. But as the September 19, 1885, issue of the *Bayfield County Press* told the story, a gale intervened and changed everything.

"Saturday morning of last week Lightkeeper Lederlee of Sand Island light, discovered a large boat on fire about ten miles off that point," said the newspaper, which spelled the keeper's name as "Lederlee" throughout the piece. In the midst of a gale blowing from the southeast, Lederle set sail in his boat for the burning vessel. Several miles out, he came upon a metallic lifeboat containing the captain, mate, engineer and fireman, all headed for shore. Those in the lifeboat told Lederle the remaining six men and one woman who had been on the steamer now were in a yawl boat being carried out into the stormy lake.

Apostle Islands National Lakeshore

Photo at left shows Emmanuel Luick and his first wife, Ella, in a formal portrait taken around 1896. At right, Luick is show with his second wife, Oramill, and one of their children, on a visit to the Raspberry Island Lighthouse.

Lederle headed out into the lake until he reached the yawl boat, whose occupants all had given up hope of reaching land. The keeper brought them into his boat, headed back to shore, and picked up those on the lifeboat. Back at the lighthouse, Lederle and his wife provided food and shelter for the eleven rescued crew members of the *Prussia* until the storm died down the next day.

"Mr. Lederlee's promptness in going to the relief of the crew can not be too highly commended and is worthy of substantial recognition by the Life Saving Service," the *Bayfield County Press* opined.

The crew of the *Prussia* offered its own view of the rescue in this letter to the keeper:

Sand Island, Wis., Sept. 12, 1885.
To the Light-house Keeper:
Dear Sir:
We the undersigned crew of the propeller Prussia, feel it is our duty to express our gratitude to you and your wife, as keeper of the Sand Island light-house, for kindness and assistance shown towards us while remaining at your house. We also wish to thank Mr. Lederlee for going to the rescue of the yawl boat and crew, as if he had not done so they would most likely have been lost, as there was a heavy sea running from the south east and they were unable to pull up against it.

Twenty years later, the ending was much less happy for the *Sevona*.

The steamer left West Superior, Wisc., shortly after 6 PM on September 1, 1905 with a load of about 6,000 tons of iron ore. The wind started to pick up around 9 PM By midnight, a gale-force wind made it clear the twenty-four on board were in the midst of a northeaster. By about 2 AM, the steamer's captain presumed he was well past Sand Island, and he decided to turn southwest and seek shelter in the Apostles. Then shortly before 6 AM, the *Sevona* struck the Sand Island shoals, one and one-half miles northeast of the Sand Island Lighthouse, and broke into two pieces.

In the stern were seventeen people and both lifeboats. In nightmarish escapes from death through the stormy waters, one boat made its way to the mainland and the other to the beach at Sand Island.

The seven crew members in the bow section were not as fortunate. Luick watched through his binoculars as the men launched their little raft, held on desperately, and closed in on Sand Island. But as they neared the beach, Luick saw huge breakers tear the raft to pieces.

This time, a keeper of the Sand Island Lighthouse could not play the hero by setting off in a boat to rescue those in the water. The violence of the storm meant all Luick could do was to stay at his station and pray.

The wreck of the *Sevona* was a high point in the life of Emmanuel Luick, who was born in Cleveland in 1866, and joined the Lighthouse Service at the age of twenty as assistant keeper of the Outer Island Lighthouse in the Apostle Islands group. He held that job for five years before he was named keeper at Sand Island in 1892. At Sand Island, he married sixteen-year-old Ella Gertrude Richardson of Smithfield, R.I., in 1896. After Ella Luick faithfully performed the duties of a keeper's wife for nearly a decade, she left the island and her husband in 1905. For reasons that no one knows, the childless couple divorced in 1906. Luick married again in 1911 and fathered four children, only two of whom lived past infancy.

The automation of the Sand Island Lighthouse was hardly the end of Luick's career. He transferred to the Grand Marais Lighthouse in Minnesota, where he retired in 1936. Luick died eleven years later in Superior, Wisc.

To that very end, it is easy to imagine, Luick may have held on to the memory of watching seven men clinging to a raft, knowing there was nothing he could do to save them.

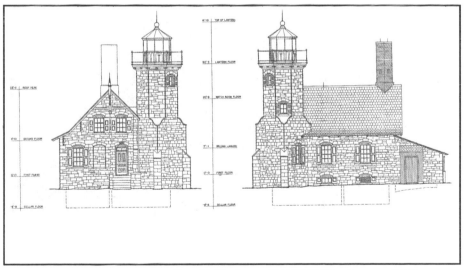

Gary R. Stephens - HABS/HAER - Summer 1989
Sand Island Light Station - Lighthouse and Keeper's Quarters

Chapter Seven
Devils Island:
A "Landmark"
in Western Lake Superior

It should be enough to say the Devils Island Lighthouse keeps watch over the northernmost point in Wisconsin, just as the lights at Montauk Point and West Quoddy Head stand at the easternmost points in New York and Maine, respectively.

And it should be enough to say mariners in sailboats and fishing boats can see the solar-powered beacon flashing from the lighthouse fifteen statute miles away. That the station has been a primary turning point on Lake Superior since a light first went on at Devils on September 30, 1891, also should give it special significance.

Local residents enjoy speaking about the successful fight they waged early in the 1990s to bring the original 3rd Order Fresnel lens back to the Devil's Island Light tower. They speak fondly of the day in 1928 when a president came to have a picnic lunch on the rock ledges southeast of the light station.

But what often enchants people the most about the place is its mystery.

Local folklore has it that of all the twenty-two Apostle Islands, Devils Island was the only one where the Ojibway (Chippewa) Indians would not bring their canoes for fear of the spirits the island might contain.

It is uncertain whether the tale originated in the mind of a local storyteller or actually reflected the practice of the early Native American population. Bob Mackreth, historian for the Apostle Islands National Lakeshore, has researched the issue, and hesitates to offer an opinion either way.

"Tradition holds that the name of Devils Island reflects the beliefs of the people who were here before even the French. The booming of the waves in the island's caves is held to produce a sound that the Ojibway interpreted as the cries of evil spirits," Mackreth has written.

However, one possibly authoritative source indicates the story goes back at least a century. In 1903, Samuel Fifield, writer and statesman, recounted this tradition in his Story of the Apostles.

"During terrible storms that periodically sweep over the great chain of lakes, these caverns become seething cauldrons and the rushing waves dash into them with almost resistless power. Often, when the storms are at their height, the roar of rushing waters is like deafening thunder, and the island itself is shaken to its very foundations. The Indians in the early days declared it to be the home of Matchie-Manitou, the Evil Spirit, whom Kitchie-Manitou, the Great Spirit, had imprisoned there; hence its name, Devils Island."

There are obvious reasons why a listener would believe the tale. For the storms that pound the island have undercut the sandstone on the island's northern end with sea caves and blow holes that give off ghostly sounds indeed when the climate is right.

The sea caves are on the northern end of a bean-shaped island, which extends one and one-quarter miles north to south and one-half mile east to west. An eighty-two-foot steel cylinder tower erected in 1898 stands near the northern end of the island, as do two two-story Queen Anne-style brick keepers' dwellings, a fog whistle building and other smaller structures.

It would be natural that anyone coming ashore in the past, and hearing the noise from the caves on a stormy night might believe the source is a sinister spirit.

No matter what people called it in the distant past, and no matter what the reason, the attraction remains for Lois Spangle. Her father, Alphonse L. Gustafson, was an assistant keeper at the Devils Island Lighthouse from 1945 until he suffered a fatal heart attack on April 29, 1951.

When Spangle came to the island, she recalls, her father told her there would be strange sounds. But he told her not to be afraid. "When we went fishing, he said, `Let's go into this (cave).' And when we went in there, I was just fascinated at the sound. I can't explain it really. It was weird, but yet it was beautiful. We knew it was Mother Nature," she said.

Kayakers today venture out to the sea caves to hear the sounds.

But there was more than the sounds that today provide sweet memories for Spangle. She recalls that a Coast Guard cutter would come from Duluth at the opening of the Lake Superior navigation season in mid-April to take keepers to their respective stations in the islands.

"Devils Island was all so very hard to reach. Even now it is for landings. But in April, there was the ice, all against the rocks and everything. They had to dynamite the ice off of the rocks to get the men onto the ramp there, and then for them to get them up to the command car with their luggage and their food and everything for them to go to their dwelling," Spangle said.

"It was a very very hard thing every year to get up to the dwelling," said Spangle, who also has memories of her father's service at the LaPointe (Long Island) Light Station in the Apostles and at Portage Lake Ship Canal Lighthouse at Houghton, Mich.

The Devils Island Light Station first was illuminated in 1891.

Hans Christensen, who was keeper at the Devils Island Light Station from 1925 to 1934, enjoys a break with some feathered friends.

"Mother Nature provided me with many entertainments and toys," she said, mentioning her collections of butterflies and wildflowers. Now a great-grandmother, she lives in Lake Delta, ten miles east of Iron River, Wisc. She shares her memories in talks with schoolchildren, church groups and historical organizations and in an informal group of keeper's children she has joined.

The thought of keeping such memories alive may have been what inspired residents of the Apostle Islands area to wage a successful battle to bring back the 3rd Order Fresnel lens first installed in the tower in 1901.

That 3rd Order lens was installed thirteen years after the Vessel Owners Association of Cleveland asked for a red flashing 3rd Order Fresnel light and fog signal in 1888. Congress appropriated $20,500 for a light and fog signal in 1890, but it was clearly inadequate for the steel light tower people wanted.

But it was enough for a temporary wooden tower, which beamed a red 4th Order lens from the shores of Devils Island on September 30, 1891. While the permanent tower was erected in 1898, delays meant the requested 3rd Order lens didn't come until 1901.

Forty inches or so in diameter and about six feet tall, the lens was and is a marvel. "That lens to my mind is just a fantastic work of art," Mackreth said. "We almost lost it."

When the station in 1978 became the last in the Apostles to be automated, the Fresnel lens remained. But in 1989, the Coast Guard decided to replace it with the small, efficient unit and dismantled the original 3rd Order Fresnel lens.

"There was a bit of controversy over it, and eventually, after a group of citizens went to court, the Coast Guard was compelled to return the lens to the National Park Service, and we arranged to have the lens reinstalled," Mackreth said.

Prior to that reinstallation in 1992, Greg Byrne, an objects conservator for the National Park Service in Harpers Ferry, W. Va., worked seven days a week for three weeks to repair damage done to the lens. Then helicopters from the National Guard brought dozens of wooden packing crates back to Devils Island, where a boom system was set up to raise the pieces to the lantern room.

"It was quite an exhilarating experience, to put it mildly, leaning out over the balcony and trying to guide some of these heavy pieces into the lighthouse," Mackreth said. The automated beacon still provides the light for passing ships and sailboats. But Mackreth said, "We got the lens back together, and it's a point of pride for all of us that the 3rd Order Fresnel lens is back in the tower at Devils, where it belongs."

Apostle Islands National Lakeshore

Hans Christensen, who was keeper of the Devils Island Light Station from 1925 to 1934, and his wife Anna.

The exhilaration they felt may have been like that experienced on the day President Calvin Coolidge came for a picnic lunch on Devils Island, on August 22, 1928, along with an entourage that included local dignitaries, cameramen, reporters and guests.

President Coolidge's day trip to the Apostles and his luncheon came near the end of a three-month summer vacation in northern Wisconsin after he had chosen not to run for re-election. The president and the party viewed the sea caves, watched a fisherman lift fish from a net and then got off on a narrow ledge of rock southeast of the light station, according to Guy M. Burnham in the 1929 book, *The Lake Superior Country in History and in Story.*

"At Devil's Island, at the extreme northwest of the (Apostle) group, the first stop of the cruise was made, the party landing at 1 p.m. for luncheon in a grove on a prominence of land affording an uninterrupted view of the vast expanse of lake," said an account in *The New York Times* the following day.

"High above the sandstone formations on the island the lighthouse-keeper and his family waved an American flag, welcoming the President," Burnham wrote. "The big fog horn, like some gigantic animal roared an almost continuous welcome, seeming almost to split the air above the pines which like an army of green spears cover the north end of Devil's Island."

Burnham reported that the president toured and inspected the lighthouse, before signing his name in the journal of Hans F. Christensen, the keeper at Devils Island. "'It's the first time in my four years here or my 12 years at Eagle Harbor, Michigan that anything so great has happened,' Captain Christensen enthused," Burnham's book said, before adding, "He declared he would write to his inspector, telling him that the lighthouse had been inspected and OK'ed by the President of the United States himself."

Born in Denmark on June 23, 1878, Christensen was Devils Island keeper from April 1925 to April 1934. He started sailing when he was fourteen, came to America later in his teens, sailed on the Great Lakes and then served on a ship in Santiago, Cuba, in the Spanish American War. He became an assistant keeper at Split Rock, Minn., around 1911 and assistant keeper at Two Harbors, Minn., around 1912. He was named first assistant keeper at Eagle Harbor, Mich., in 1913 and transferred to Devils in 1925.

Christensen and his wife, Anna, also a Danish immigrant, had three children. Anna died at the age of 80 in 1961 and Hans at 89 in 1968. Both are buried at Eagle Harbor, on the Upper Peninsula of Michigan, not far from the Great Lake where they spent much of their lives.

At the end of his life, it's possible Hans Christensen would have agreed with the words of Lois Spangle when she said, "It was a great life, I will say. I'm happy with my heritage."

Ghostly and beautiful sounds sometimes come from the sea caves at the northern end of Devils Island.

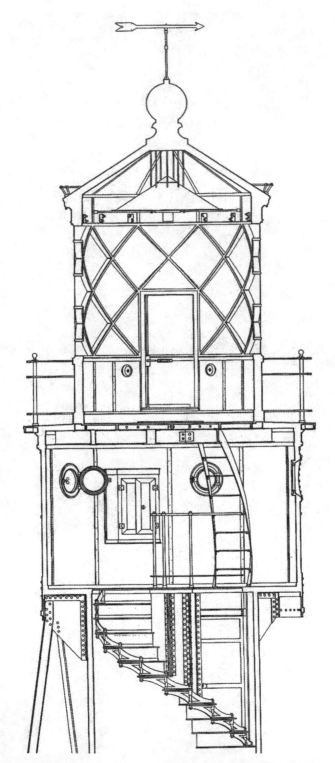

Gillian Lewis - HABS/HAER - Summer 1991
The lantern room and watch room of the Devils Island Light Station tower.

Chapter Eight
Ashland Harbor Breakwater Light:
Beacon at the End of the Line

As a youngster, Donna Peterson could look onto the lake from her house and see Bayfield, Washburn, some islands and ships coming into Ashland. There was beauty in the view, but also a source of worry when the weather turned ugly.

Peterson was one of four children of Frank Mersy, who was keeper of the Ashland Harbor Breakwater Light from 1925 until he retired in 1951. From the family's house on the shore, Mersy had to make a daily two-mile trip by boat to the breakwater light.

"When he'd go out there, in storms and what-not, everybody was pressing their nose to the window, waiting for him to come back, because the lake got really rough," said Peterson.

For shippers coming into Ashland and Washburn, Mersy's light was a beacon at the end of the line, after they passed the lighthouses of the Apostle Islands, and entered Chequamegon Bay.

In this role, it showed that it both is and isn't one of the lights of the Apostle Islands region.

"It's not one of the islands, but it is one of what I would call the Apostles group. It's one of the seven light stations in the region," said Dave Snyder, former historian for the Apostle Islands National Lakeshore, and the historian of the U.S. Lighthouse Society.

"Anyone that came by boat into Ashland would either have gone by the Long Island Light or by the Sand Island Light, because there wasn't any way to get through there other than going by some of the lighthouses," Snyder said. "The whole reason for all those lighthouses in the Apostles, except for external navigation, changes in Lake Superior and stuff, was basically to guide people through those islands into the ports of Ashland and Washburn."

"You can see the Apostle Islands from here," said Dick Anderson, who volunteers with his wife for the Ashland Historical Society and its museum. "It's not part of the islands, but of course the lighthouses are out there because of the boats that came into Ashland."

Ore boats, coal boats and pulpwood rafts combined to keep the port of Ashland busy, said Anderson, a retired schoolteacher and administrator who delivered dry cleaning to Mersy's house around 1950. "They thought at one time that Ashland was going to be the biggest port on the Great Lakes," Anderson said.

With the booming shipping trade, the city's early leaders laid out plans for a town big enough for 100,000 people. But when the trees were all cut and the area's iron ore mines were emptied, the trade ended.

Today, most of the shipping is gone, and guides to the Apostle Islands lighthouses usually do not include the Ashland Harbor Breakwater Light. Travelers driving on U.S. Highway 2 through Ashland on their way to the Apostle Islands lights come within sight of it, but may be in too much of a hurry to stop to take a look.

That would be a mistake. The complete visit to the lighthouses out on the islands starts by finding an open area along the shore to take a good look at Ashland Harbor's light.

In some ways, the Ashland Harbor Breakwater Light is like Roger Maris, the New York Yankees slugger who hit sixty-one home runs in 1961, breaking Babe Ruth's record of sixty homers made in 1927. In the record books, an asterisk popped up next to Maris' name, pointing to a notation that Maris needed 162 games to break the record, eight more than Ruth had when he hit sixty.

Whatever mark stood beside his name, the single-season record belonged to Maris. So it is with the Ashland Harbor Breakwater Light. No matter what the tour books say, any discussion of the Apostle Islands lighthouses is incomplete if it leaves out the one at Ashland. Nonetheless, the breakwater light remains an important local attraction in Ashland.

"People are very curious of course about the lighthouse and will stop and ask questions," said Mary McPhetridge, executive director of the Ashland Area Chamber of Commerce.

"I think it's very popular because you can see it from our entire shoreline of Chequamegon Bay," said Maribeth Monroe, who does public relations for the Ashland Area Chamber of Commerce. "It's absolutely beautiful."

Located near the east side of town, on the east side of the ore dock, the light is a favorite place for fishing, Monroe said.

"It definitely has a tourist attraction to it," Monroe said.

"People do stop to take a look at it as they're coming in from the east, because it is very noticeable," Monroe said. "Even if it isn't on their maps or they're headed to the Apostle Islands, it still very much catches their attention. . . .There are spots where they can pull their cars over and check out the lighthouse."

The Ashland Harbor Breakwater Light was lit in 1915, replacing a light that had been in operation since 1911. While not an Apostle Islands station, it is an important part of the system of lights around the Apostle Islands region.

Monroe and her husband, Edward, a boating enthusiast and Ashland community leader, love to head out to the shore to enjoy the scenery, including the lighthouse. "It just accentuates Lake Superior."

The white hexagonal pyramid-style lighthouse is best seen from the east side of town. The fifty-eight-foot tower is at the far northwestern end of a one-and-a-half-mile-long breakwater designed to soften the blow from waves stirred up by winds from the northeast.

In many other port towns, breakwaters reached to the shore, enabling keepers who lived on the shore to walk to work. But there was no sidewalk for keepers at Ashland. At its closest point, the breakwater comes within a half-mile of the shore on the east side of Ashland. Although there was a keeper's dwelling within sight of the light on shore, their commute still was by boat.

Peterson recalls that while the light came on automatically every day, Mersy still went out there almost every day to check on things. "If the weather was bad, he wouldn't go out," she said. Often though, he would venture out in uneasy weather.

When storms came up and Mersy couldn't get back, he would stay in the living quarters at the station, which came complete with a kitchen and a bedroom. Sometimes the whole Mersy family stayed there. Her friends thought that was neat.

In the winter, when the lake froze, the light stayed on. Peterson's father went out every two or three days. He pushed a sled on the ice that also served as a boat when the ice broke.

There were three levels to the lighthouse, Peterson said.

"The first floor was the engine room. The second floor was the kitchen and then the third floor was the bedroom, with the light," Peterson said.

"The storm would come up when he would be out there, although there were living quarters there and he stayed out there quite a bit, too." Peterson said.

"He had a radio station. He had to check all the other islands, all the other lighthouses on the Apostle Islands. He had to call in every morning and every night," said Peterson, who raised her family in Ashland, and still takes boat rides around the light in the summer.

During World War II, Mersy had the added duty of fingerprinting people, for a reason Peterson never quite understood.

"He just got a letter saying that certain people should be fingerprinted and that's what he did. For what reason, I don't know. Everything was so top secret then, you know," said Peterson.

Peterson's father began serving ten years after the present light went into operation.

An item in the *Ashland Daily Press* on September 24, 1915, brought news that the Chequamegon Bay–Ashland Breakwater Light Station permanent light and fog signal would be established around the middle of the next month.

The article in the *Ashland Daily Press* noted that the station would have a continuous cycle of white light for two seconds, followed by a second of darkness. The 4th Order Fresnel lens would show forth 1,600 candlepower, on a pyramidal tower on pierhead.

The fog signal would be an electric siren, with a four-second blast, followed by sixteen seconds of silence. A temporary light built four years earlier would be disconnected on the same date.

Today, the Coast Guard's task is much simpler than the one Peterson's father had. A crew from the Guard's Aids to Navigation Team from Duluth, Minn., stops by once a year for a half hour or so to check the solar-powered automated light and make sure it will stay in operation for another year.

The lighthouse is not the most handsome one the Guard may come across.

"It's just like a cement structure," said First Class Boatswain's Mate Kevin Kleisath, executive petty officer of the Duluth Aids to Navigation Team. "Right now, there's nothing in there except some stairs. . . . There's not a whole lot up there."

It's one of two lights on either end of the breakwater.

"The shore side has got a small red light, and the lighthouse of course has got a real bright light on it," Edward Monroe said.

Unlike many other lighthouses, this one was not built to warn mariners to stay away from natural hazards. It went up to keep them clear of a man-made dangerous object, the Ashland Harbor Breakwater.

"They wouldn't have had to have a light out there if there would have been no hazard, but they built a breakwall to protect the harbor," Edward Monroe said.

But something is needed to hold down the effect of winds that come howling from the northeast, stirring up waves.

"The breakwall sticks out of the water, probably a good ten feet or so," said Monroe, who has often gone out to see the breakwater and the lighthouse in his inboard-outboard boat. "It's all large brownstone and granite rocks."

In the days when big ore boats came into Ashland, the lighthouse was a beacon for them. It helps larger vessels to find their way into the shipping channel that extends from Long Island to Ashland, Monroe said.

"Without the breakwater, the waves coming from out of the bay would be six or eight foot waves lapping in to the shoreline," Monroe said. The breakwater reduces the waves to about two feet. "So it's relatively calm on the bay side," he said.

"The lighthouse marks where you've got to start to turn," Monroe said. "It's kind of a fixture you look at, you look for, a light when you're coming in at night."

"It's home to hundreds of seagulls, terns and cormorants now," Monroe said. "It used to be almost entirely seagulls."

On stormy days, people weren't thinking about birds.

"There were people that drowned out there," Peterson said.

"A lot of ore boats would come in and people that worked on the ore boats would fall in the water and stuff, and he'd have to go and drag for them. It was pretty rough some times," Peterson said of her father's work.

Being a lighthouse keeper's daughter causes mixed thoughts for Peterson. "It brings back good memories and bad memories. There was a lot of worry."

Chapter Nine
Apostle Islands Lighthouse Celebration: See You in September

Four-year-old Zack Leslie thought he was just out for a trip on a boat and a visit to an island with his parents one sunny day in September 1999.

In truth, Zack was coming down with the lighthouse bug. One of the youngest participants in the Fourth Annual Apostle Islands Lighthouse Celebration, the preschooler had just come ashore on Outer Island. There he would climb with his parents, Mary and Karl Leslie, to the very top of the Outer Island Lighthouse to get a good view of the western end of Lake Superior.

"My wife is a lighthouse junkie," said Karl, an attorney. "It's really a contagious thing."

There was lots of that contagion in evidence for three weeks in the Apostle Islands in September 1999, as there has been at every Apostle Islands Lighthouse Celebration since the first one in 1996.

Since the beginning, the lighthouse celebration has been a way to welcome thousands of visitors to lights they otherwise could not visit. It has given a whole new meaning to the old song, "See You in September."

"We start Wednesday after Labor Day, because the Apostle Islands Cruise Service ends all their other cruises (Labor Day) and this is the time that their boats are free to do something like this," said Mary Grant, manager of the Keeper of the Light gift shop in Bayfield, which sponsors the lighthouse celebration. The cruise service's summer itinerary includes a daily "Grand Tour" through the islands, as well as scheduled trips to islands and past lighthouses. But generally, there are only regular summertime stops at two lighthouses, on Raspberry and Sand islands. "So unless you have your own boat or your own way to get out there, you can't go see those lighthouses," Grant said.

By contrast, the schedule of the Lighthouse Celebration includes stops at all six of the Apostle Islands National Lakeshore light stations and a cruise by the Ashland Harbor Breakwater Light.

"A lot of people that come around here don't even know these lighthouses are out here," Grant said. "It definitely is a growing interest."

The lake waters sometimes are rougher in September than in the summertime. The lighthouses are in exposed areas, usually with poor docking facilities. Sometimes, bad weather forced a cancellation, or high waves made it impossible to complete a transfer between a cruise vessel to a water taxi that would bring people to islands with lighthouses. "Old Mother Nature, we have to contend with her, and that's all there is to it," Grant said.

"Every year it differs. Every year it changes," Dave Strzok, owner of the Keeper of the Light gift shop and the Apostle Islands Cruise Service, told those attending the keeper's dinner in 2000. To those attending the main event of that year's lighthouse celebration, he stressed the need to protect visitors. "We have to make these decisions about safety, so if you don't get out there, it's for a good reason."

Even when there is a cancellation, there is still plenty to do for lighthouse celebrants left on shore. On a day full of drizzles, there are places in downtown Bayfield with just the right kind of coffee to warm the body and make the traveler ready to hunt for bargains in the shops.

Those who plan the Lighthouse Celebration also have a wide variety of onshore activities.

The highlight is the keeper's dinner held at the Bayfield Waterfront Pavilion next to the city dock.

Past speakers have included Lee Radzak, site manager of the Split Rock Lighthouse at the western end of Lake Superior; and James R. Marshall, who is considered to be the leading authority on Lake Superior. Marshall is the chairman of Lake Superior Port Cities, Inc., which publishes *Lake Superior Magazine,* and the author of a popular column for that magazine.

"The interesting thing about lighthouses is that they have to be put in place because of commercial traffic to begin with," Marshall said, in a wide-ranging speech about Lake Superior given at the 2000 keeper's dinner. "And the commercial traffic on Lake Superior had many different reasonings and sources as it began."

During the same dinner, the author gave a dramatic telling of his story, *An Unexpected Visitor,* which is reprinted elsewhere. He also signed copies of the initial rough edition of this book. The year before he told another story based on the same characters. Both stories are in a novel he is writing that's based on the Devils Island Light Station.

Among those who have attended keeper's dinners are several people who lived at Apostle Islands lighthouses. They were Robert E. Parker, Sr. who served at the Long Island and Outer Island light stations in the 1940s and 1950s, Lois Spangle, whose father served at Apostle Islands lights from the 1930s to 1951, and Jean Brander, whose husband served on lighthouses from 1922 to 1948. Brander's son, Robert, also attended.

Karl and Mary Leslie enjoy a moment with their son Zack at the top of the Outer Island Lighthouse tower, in a visit during the Apostle Islands Lighthouse Celebration.

During lighthouse celebrations, the Apostle Islands National Lakeshore Visitor Center also offered presentations on subjects that ranged from the history of the Apostle Islands lighthouses to light-houses in movies.

Other activities for the event have included a concert by Lee Murdock, a musician who specializes in Great Lakes music. Artist Randall Peterson, a lighthouse artist who uses the technique called pointillism, and woodcarver Kevin Midthun also made appearances. Award-winning master photographer Dale Thomas gave instructions about lighthouse photography.

As busy as a lighthouse celebrant may be on shore, the ultimate goal remains the Apostle Islands lighthouses.

"I just like the nostalgic part of it. I think about the keepers that used to live out here," said Mary Leslie, a schoolteacher and the mother of the aforementioned Zackary Leslie.

Zackary Leslie decided it was too much to go up the big tower on Michigan Island. He said "That was too scary," his mom said, after a visit to Outer and Michigan Islands. While Zack refused to go up that one tower, he still busied himself with an activity enjoyed by many a keeper and his family: playing croquet.

Two others on the same cruise to Outer and Michigan Islands were Deb and Jim Meyer of Madison, Wisc.

"We've been coming since the start of the lighthouse festival. Actually, we come up every year for Apple Fest," Deb Meyer said, referring to a popular event in Bayfield every October. "Once they started the lighthouse festival, then we started coming up for that as well . . . . My husband actually is the lighthouse nut. He got me into them as well, a little bit. We just love seeing old lighthouses and they fascinate us."

Deb's husband, Jim, also used the word "lighthouse nut" to describe himself. "The lore of what these people went through out on these islands, the hardships and yet the satisfaction of being in a position to save lives by their work really interests me," he said. "I'm very much a history buff. And that's what this is."

Four others who came to indulge their devotion to lighthouses were Dennis and Mary Myers of Milwaukee, Wisc., and Gary and Sue Hammond of Cambridge, Wisc. Like many of those who came to the Lighthouse Celebration, these are not merely people who think a picture of a lighthouse is pretty.

"When I married him, I married lighthouses also," Mary Myers said of her husband. "I never even gave them a thought before that. They are fascinating. I think what I enjoy most about them are the stories, the people that lived in them, and the history behind them is what fascinates me," said Myers, a receptionist and a secretary in a doctor's office.

During the Apostle Islands Lighthouse Celebration, a boat takes passengers transferred from a larger vessel to the small dock at the Outer Island Light Station.

As for the reason Mary Myers wanted to get near the lighthouses of the Apostles, she said, "I'm just interested in seeing them, rather than just drive by with the boats."

Myers' husband, Dennis, who works in facilities and maintenance for the Milwaukee Public Schools, said he's been around lighthouses in Florida, Virginia, Michigan and Wisconsin. He said the two were in the Bayfield area years earlier and took a boat excursion past the islands, but never had a chance to see the lighthouses close up. "This gives us a chance to actually go on to the lighthouses. You can get the beauty and mystique of the place," he said.

The Hammonds, who operate a restaurant and retail shops in Cambridge, Wisc., offered similar reasons for coming.

"We've always liked lighthouses. We thought it would be kind of fun to actually walk up and if we can go upstairs, we'll do that or whatever we can do," Gary Hammond said. Of all the lighthouses of the Apostles, he likes the architecture of the native sandstone Gothic Revival-style structure on the north end of Sand Island.

But people come to Bayfield and come to the Lighthouse Celebration for more reasons than to hear about shipwrecks or even – is it possible? – lighthouses.

"I'm really here because of the Great Lakes. I love the water, and the lighthouses are just the frosting on the cake," Sue Hammond said. "I think we've probably been in the Bayfield area about six different times. We just really are attracted to the Great Lakes. I grew up on Lake Superior. So we always kind of come back to the Great Lakes, mainly Superior and Michigan. We love the boats, just everything that the water brings."

As people like the Myers and the Hammonds began coming to the celebration, its length expanded. It went from a week-long event in 1998 to three weeks in 1999. In 2000, there were a total of ninety-six scheduled trips.

This did more than increase attendance.

"A couple years before, we'd see the same people throughout the event," Grant said. Now there are many new people, she said.

"The whole crowd tonight practically was brand new. That's a good sign," Strzok said after the end of the 1999 keeper's dinner. "It was designed to be a cycle, and they get opportunities to do other and different things. It seems to be working that way."

Among those attracted to a longer celebration were Roger and Pam Mueller of Rochester, Minn., who came with their nineteen-month-old son, Graham. Asked why she liked lighthouses, Pam said, "They're beautiful, kind of a wonderful piece of history, romantic, just real pretty."

Mary McNab of Rochester, Minn., a friend of the Muellers, said of lighthouses, "I think they're just beautiful, kind of the beacon of light and the whole symbolism of keeping people safe, coming into shore." She said this was her first visit to the Apostle Islands. "It's been very interesting just to see the area and see the lighthouses here."

Eric M. Wefelmeyer, a computer operator from Minneapolis, Minn., was in his element at the 2000 Annual Apostle Islands Lighthouse Celebration. Wefelmeyer said he would have enjoyed being a lighthouse keeper, if he'd been born earlier. "I've always enjoyed the solitude aspect of the job," he said. "I've always been fairly much one to function on my own and go on my own directions, and the idea of living that lifestyle was appealing."

Chapter Ten
Keeping the Light Under the Big Top

From the Sand Island Lighthouse, some can visualize what it was like for keeper Emmanuel Luick to watch as the steamer *Sevona* broke up in a storm, killing seven people.

The story of Luick's helplessness as he watched the destruction of the *Sevona* on September 2, 1905, is a mainstay of the lore around the six light stations of the Apostle Islands of Lake Superior. While some only need to stand where Luick stood to catch the drama of that moment, there is one method guaranteed to give even the most stony-hearted the sense of the turmoil that gripped Luick for years after he watched the death struggle of the *Sevona*.

That is a ticket to see *Keeper of the Light,* a musical and dramatic celebration of the lighthouses, keepers and keepers' families in the Apostle Islands, presented yearly at the Lake Superior Big Top Chautauqua just outside Bayfield. It's one of several house shows about local, regional and state history put on at the 780-seat tent theater.

The shows are squeezed into an eclectic summer season that also may feature nationally recognized performers like Merle Haggard, Garrison Keillor, Willie Nelson and Gordon Lightfoot.

Keeper is a yearly mainstay of the house shows. It allows those watching under the tent to eavesdrop as Luick gets a visit from a *Detroit News* reporter not long before transfer to the Grand Marais Light in Minnesota in 1921.

Asked to offer some memories of his twenty-nine years on Sand Island, Luick begins to tell the tale of that night in September 1905, fifteen years before the reporter's visit. From then, the viewer is taken in. He sees as the *Sevona* gets caught in a storm, the passengers leave, and seven crew members drown in their raft.

The scene is one of many in the musical play, crafted by Warren Nelson, producer, artistic director and resident writer for Big Top Chautauqua. Nelson researched it with Betty Ferris, the other half of the Nelson-Ferris Concert Company.

It's not necessary to attend performances of *Keeper of the Light* to get a taste of it. There is a tape and CD of much of the musical parts. In addition, it's hard for the visitor to avoid hearing music from it, because it's played in shops in downtown Bayfield.

Lake Superior Big Top Chautauqua
A scene from Keeper of the Light.

Keeper of the Light has captivated audiences ever since its first performance in 1989.

"It's one of our most important shows," said Carolyn Sneed, executive director of Lake Superior Big Top Chautauqua, and one of the founders back in 1986. "The audience has been growing for it every year."

The story of *Keeper of the Light* actually starts in 1976, when Nelson wrote and produced a historical illustrated musical called *A Martin County Hornpipe,* using songs, poetry, old photographs and narratives to tell the story of his hometown, Fairmount, Minn. In that, Nelson worked with several of the people still associated with Big Top Chautauqua, including Ferris.

The success of that play led to a commission for the Nelson-Ferris Concert Company to research and produce *Souvenir Views,* a centennial musical about Washburn, a town just down the road from Bayfield.

Another commission to produce *Riding the Wind,* a musical about Bayfield, followed. In 1986, Nelson's dream of a tent theater in the spirit of the old traveling tent chautauquas became a reality, with Lake Superior Big Top Chautauqua.

Other illuminated musical histories followed. Then Warren Nelson and Big Top Chautauqua were asked to produce something to celebrate the two-hundreth anniversary of the U.S. Lighthouse Service in 1989.

The players in Keeper of the Light sing a song in honor of lighthouses.

"With Bayfield having been chosen, it was just a natural that we should do a musical about the history (of lighthouses)," said Phillip Anich, operations manager for Big Top Chautauqua, and a singer and player in *Keeper of the Light.*

To do his research, Nelson referred to libraries, history books, old journals and oral histories with elders who live in the area and who were lighthouse keepers or lived with lighthouse keepers.

"I am a freshwater man," Nelson said. He got interested in lighthouses "because of the lights on the Apostle Islands, and really, this show woke me up to lighthouses."

There's several things Nelson enjoys about this production, including the darkness that balances the light, the fear of the lake and the beacon.

"A fair amount of material actually came from the journals of the keepers themselves," Anich said.

For the lighthouse enthusiast, Nelson notes several things that would make the production appealing.

Those include the "very real portraits of those who lived on the lights, and the frightening part of why lighthouses were needed," Nelson said, mentioning shipwrecks like the one on the *Sevona.*

In his writing, Nelson did not avoid the negative side of lighthouse keeping.

Lake Superior Big Top Chautauqua
Keeper of the Light is one of several popular house shows performed yearly at Lake Superior Big Top Chautauqua.

Although the play tells about a young girl who fell in love with life at a real place with a storybook name like Raspberry Island, it also offers an unromanticized view of life at another place called Devils Island. In the most fanciful view of lighthouses, everyone loved life at lighthouses. In truth, Nelson's portrayal of a keeper on Devils Island whose wife hated his work shows how many reacted.

That keeper with the wife who hates life on Devils Island is portrayed by Anich.

"We've put that in as really a slice of reality," Anich said. "It certainly was a hard existence for a lot of people."

There have been a fair amount of people in audiences who actually were children of keepers, Anich said. "We've had direct links of people who remember that. They get very nostalgic."

It helps that such a production is shown to the public a short boat ride from six lighthouses.

"We have many visitors who come here specifically for the light-houses," said Nicole Wilde, former marketing director for Big Top Chautauqua. "This really digs a little deeper. . . . Here's some real stories that really happened."

Among those telling the story is Geoff Ehrendreich, who has been a player in Keeper for several years.

"I never thought about the regimen of the light work. Wake up early in the morning and scrub the place from top to bottom," Ehrendreich said.

"It's always been well received. A lot of people, they come up and they do the lighthouse tours," Ehrendreich said. "It's a nice way to start or wind down the lighthouse experience."

Chapter Eleven
Happy Memories: The Story of One Keeper's Daughter

For Ed Lane, his wife, Elizabeth, and their four children, life was full of flower gardens, songs about a lighthouse keeper's daughter and beams from the Michigan Island Light Station.

Lane was keeper at Michigan Island from 1902 until 1939, making him the longest-serving keeper in the Apostle Islands. From stories told by a daughter years later, an image emerges of an idyllic existence, the kind one imagines for inhabitants of the lighthouses in paintings sold in gift shops.

"We children never missed playmates — Mom and Dad played with us and formed teams," Edna Lane Sauer recalled, nearly half a century after her father's retirement. "So many happy memories of those days — never was lonely — just too busy working and playing."

Before her death in 1991 in Moline, Ill., at the age of ninety-six, Sauer provided a vivid portrayal of the happy life of a family that seemed perfect for the isolated life at a light station.

"It's not the typical kind of life that one would have living in a town," said Bob Mackreth, historian for the Apostle Islands National Lakeshore. "Some people of course adapted well to it and others did not adapt so well. It certainly seems that the Lanes were able to adapt very well to this isolated life. . . . Edna had many pleasant memories and many fond things to say about her time at the lighthouse."

Sauer was just turning seven when the family came to the island. She attended Bayfield area schools and summered on Michigan Island until 1914. Then she developed a condition, called an "inward goiter," that made her faint and made it harder to breathe.

Told by doctors her health would improve if she lived in a warmer climate, she moved south, to Davenport, Iowa. Her health improved and she never moved back. But she often returned to visit, and shared her recollections with local residents, and later historians for the National Park Service. It is those recollections and letters she wrote that provided a clear picture of life on Michigan Island.

Sauer last returned to Bayfield in 1985, when she was ninety. Four years later, she expressed thanks to God that her mind was still clear.

I hope they (the National Park Service) refurnish Michigan Island some day, and that I can help. I know and remember every piece of furniture in my old home, even to the woodbox in the kitchen. Keeping it filled was our job! Earlier in the fall, Dad would walk out the path . . . where he would cut down the birch trees, and sawed the limbs into correct length. We children would pile them up for the winter. He always made a shelter for us of birch branches to keep us warm. Loved it!

Dave Snyder, the former historian of the Apostle Islands National Lakeshore and the historian for the U.S. Lighthouse Society, thought of visiting Sauer before she died, but never did. Nonetheless, he has strong recollections of speaking to her by phone several times.

"While she was still in her home, and then when she was in her rest home, I talked to her," Snyder said. "I talked to her maybe five or six times, and she would write me, but she wouldn't always remember that she wrote. She would write the park and she would thank us and she would say she talked to that nice guy, but she could never remember my name."

In her conversations, tapes and letters, Sauer was highly accurate, Snyder said.

"She would tell me some odd little thing and I would kind of research it and ferret it out and make a much bigger, more interesting thing out of it," Snyder said. "She had a very, very excellent memory."

Although she left Bayfield as a young child, Sauer kept up her contacts with lighthouse people.

"As a young married woman she went back to Michigan Island several time to visit her father. Then her brother was the keeper on Passage Island off Isle Royale for a time. So she would continue to be steeped in lighthouses all these years," Snyder said.

In November 1987, she provided this glimpse into food preparation at the station:

That kitchen was really something! Dad boarded up one end to make a pantry. The huge wood box stood in one corner - the wood-burning cookstove opposite it with a shelf above where the coffee mill, tea and coffee pots, canisters for tea and coffee, which we had to grind each morning - sitting on the step between dining room and kitchen. One long table against the wall with seven chairs around it [Mr. and Mrs. Lane, four kids and Grandma Lane]. One window. Black iron sink and pump in one corner - towel rack (roller towels) on wall. That was it.

In 1988, she offered this recollection, of the vegetation around the light station.

Apostle Islands National Lakeshore
Edna Lane on Michigan Island, around 1910.

There were ninety-six wooden steps coming up the hillside and ending in a small platform at the top, over head an arch of cherry tree blossoms. The cherry trees formed a "wind-break" along the top of the clay banks. Then there was a very large one beside the fancy "out-house" just a short distance from the dwelling - it was always loaded with fruit. In later years, Dad transplanted nearly a dozen trees to the meadow side of the dwelling. The meadow contained three huge crabapple trees and one pear tree which never bore fruit. Each spring Dad burned the meadow over and then it was a beautiful sight filled with yellow daisies and brown-eyed susans. A tiny streamlet ran through the meadow and over the hillside to the lake. Mom always planted a vegetable and fruit garden in part of the meadow.

Early on, Sauer's father was doing his part to save the eagles, she recalled in 1989.

There was one huge pine tree — partly on the (lighthouse grounds) that one lumber company wanted Dad to sell to them — they didn't know my Dad! That tree was where the eagles always nested. When Dad would be fishing, lifting a net, the eagle would watch him and Dad would wave a nice trout then throw it in the air. Mr. Eagle never missed it."

Sauer was not alone in her devotion to her father.

"Ed Lane was known to be a very meticulous keeper and when he retired, the district superintendent sent him a letter that said, 'Your lighthouse has been one of the showplaces of the Lighthouse Service. It's clear that it will not be able to maintain those same standards,'" Mackreth said.

The Lanes saw their love of lighthouses as an occasion for singing.

Sauer recalled her mother loved to play the guitar and sing a ballad about Grace Darling, a Victorian-era lighthouse keeper's daughter in England. Darling became famous because of her brave rescue of nine survivors of a shipwreck in the Farne Islands in England on September 7, 1838.

"They named one of their daughters Grace Darling Lane," Mackreth said. In later life, Sauer remarked that she was not sure whether her sister appreciated having the middle name Darling.

"They took their position as keepers of the light quite seriously, when they named one of their daughters after a figure from lighthouse history," Mackreth said.

There was nothing unusual or eccentric about Ed Lane, Mackreth said.

"I would put it the exact opposite," Mackreth said. "He was a very normal, stable kind of guy from every indication. You'll see evidence that there are some people who really adapt well to lighthouse life and some people who do not."

These binoculars used by Michigan Island Light Station Keeper Ed Lane are on display in the Apostle Islands National Lakeshore Visitor Center.

Some keepers fought with their assistants and some assistants quit in disgust after a year or so.

"Ed Lane and his wife, Elizabeth, they seemed to quite like lighthouse life," Mackreth said. The fact that the Lanes spent so long on the island indicates they accommodated well to it, Mackreth said.

In their thirty-seven years, the Lanes saw major changes in the routine at lighthouses. The major one, of course, was the move from the old lighthouse built in 1857.

A series of changes came to the station in 1928 and 1929. A new brick building contained an electric generator, a radio fog beacon and a hoist engine for a tramway. In 1928, the Lanes and an assistant moved to a new three-bedroom brick building.

In 1929, the station got a new, taller cylindrical steel tower for the light.

Ed Lane recorded the change from one light to another this way in his log book:

October 29, 1929 - Put window shades and worked in old tower. Started up new tower at sunset. Everything in good shape, but station looked odd.

What struck him as odd was that the old tower was dark for the first time in sixty years.

"In 1929, he would have been at that station already for twenty-seven years. That's a huge change in the routine," Mackreth said.

Lane stayed on for another ten years before his retirement. He moved to Moline, Ill., where he lived until 1949.

The end of Lane's service at Michigan Island also brought the end of an era. In the letter noting Lane's retirement, the district superintendent said the lighthouse was scheduled for automation. The process was completed by 1943.

In many ways, the Lanes represented the best of lighthouse lore. Without the willingness of Edna Lane Sauer to share her memories, we would know much less about the family's day-to-day life.

Chapter Twelve
Day to Day at a Lighthouse: The Logbook of Francis Jacker

One of the best ways to sense the day-to-day life of a lighthouse keeper is to read a logbook.

In these brief daily diaries, officially called journals, keepers recounted activities ranging from saving victims of a shipwreck to picking strawberries. The former event was rare. Usually, keepers filled the pages with the humdrum activities of a life spent making sure their lights always were on at night.

Some keepers satisfied themselves with the briefest summations of the day's activities, or even only a listing of each day's temperature. Others were more colorful.

One of the more interesting logs in the Apostle Islands was the one kept by Francis Jacker, who was keeper of the Raspberry Island Lighthouse from 1885 to 1892.

Jacker's logs covering the four years from 1887 to 1890 make note of the crops he planted in his garden, visits to the island, the weather and the deaths of two fishermen when their boat capsized. It also contains his account of a frightful experience that caused his station's light to go out for a night. The same story also is told in Chapter Four.

Below is much of Jacker's log for that period. It is presented with a minimum of editing, from a transcription on computer disk provided by the Apostle Islands National Lakeshore.

Journal of Lths Station at Raspberry Island, Lake Superior, Wis., Francis Jacker, Keeper
1887
05/08/87 Arrived at the Station in the evening and lighted the Lamp at 8 o'clock. Channel open. Fields of ice floating in the Lake. Steam barge "Vanderbuilt" is the first boat of the season from below: passed yesterday. Propeller "Winslow" first passenger boat, bound for Duluth, passed today. Weather fine, but hazy.

05/15/87 The weather for the past week was remarkably fine, but for the most time hazy. Very few boats passed as yet, with the exception of the last two days. Fields of ice still floating about, though scattering and gradually diminishing in size.

The revolving apparatus does not work regularly and stopped altogether last night. Put on additional weights which proved to be of some help. Propeller "City of Fremont" passed tonight (half-past seven), upward bound on her first semi-weekly trip.

05/22/87 Weather continued fine and dry. Ice all disappeared. Thoroughly cleansed and over-hauled apparatus which is now working well. Painted sailboat, floors of dwelling house, also out-buildings.

05/29/87 Raining today. Weather has been delightful the last four days, but rather cool.

06/17/87 Upon my arrival at the station I found the water in the well frozen into one solid piece of ice. It began and continued to melt very slowly until the last remnant of ice disappeared last night, aided by heavy and warm showers.

Wild strawberries will be plentiful this summer, a few just beginning to ripen.

06/26/87 The first part of the week past has been rainy with cold, westerly winds. Latter past, dry and clear with breezes from the easterly directions. Temperature moderately warm.

07/07/87 A very warm day. During the week past calms prevailed with occasional breezes from the west.

Rain on the Fourth. No celebration within twelve miles of the station. The day was passed in quiet solitude, as usual.

The reinstitution of an assistant keeper for this station is deemed necessary by the present writer [Jacker] for reasons submitted by letter to the inspector. In case of an emergency, no assistance is available on the island, and the proper surveillance of the revolving apparatus during the long nights of the fall when frequent windings are required, is exhausting.

07/22/87 Lt.House tender "Warrington" delivered annual supplies (2 P.M.). Comdr. H. Elmer, Inspector.

08/11/87 Tug "Daisy" (Capt. Brower) brought an excursion party who visited the station and expressed their delight over the rural attractions of the place. They were the first visitors of the season.

08/22/87 Blowing a NE gale - the first fore-runner of the equinoctial storms. Cold and cloudy fall weather.

This photo of the Raspberry Island Lighthouse, taken around 1900, shows how it looked before improvements in 1906-1907.

08/30/87

September: furious blows from the NW on the 7th, 8th, & 9th-forerunners of the equinoctial storms.

September 13th to 15th: early in the morning of the 13th, a westerly gale sprang up, all of a sudden, endangering the sailboat of the station which that night had been anchored near the dock. Jumping out of bed, I hurried to move it to a place of safety at the eastern extremity of the island - the dilapidated condition of the ways rendering it impossible, for the moment, to have it hauled up to the boathouse. In the dark, I missed the point of landing, sailing beyond it, and the impetuosity of the storm made it impossible either to row or beat up against it, gravel having entered and lodged in the centerboard box, prevented the use of the latter (the centerboard); consequently tacking could not be resorted to. I could do nothing but to sail, under reefed canvas, with the current of wind and waves, thus drifting over to Oak Island. The storm did not abate until noon of the third day, by which time the boat had received such damage that there would have been no escape for me from my prison, were it not for a passing Indian who noticed my signal of distress and rescued me. I had spent nearly three days on the desolated island, without food, without fire, and being but scantily dressed. In consequence of the above occurence, the light of this station was not extinguished in the morning of the 13th, and not exhibited the nights following. It was relighted, however, in the night of the 14th-15th by my family who happened to come on a visit, but owing to their inability to get the revolving machinery into motion, the apparatus did not revolve.

09/20/87 The inspector visited this station for the second time this season.
November: Francis Jacker, Principal Keeper
Edward Jacker, Ass't.
By authority of the Lt.House Board, an assistant has been granted this station. He arrived and commenced actual service on the 15th instant.
11/27/87 Driving snowstorm
11/27/87 Ice floating about in the channel.
11/30/87 Extinguished the light for the season.
1888
05/16/88 Arrived at the station and commenced lighting up.
Spring unusually late and channels densely covered with floating ice.
05/25/88 Plenty of ice still floating about. Weather very damp and foggy; but 2 or 3 dry days since the 16th.
06/05/88 Today and yesterday are the first warm days of the season. Ice has disappeared with the exception of a limited field visible from this station. It stretches from a point west of Sand Island into the bay opposite (Sand Bay), and is apparently solid and immovable. The fresh blow of yesterday from the south had no effect on it.
06/06/88 The above field of ice has moved out of sight.
06/14/88 Lt.House tender "Warrington" delivered annual lt.house supplies (7 A.M.). Station inspected by Commander Horace Elmer, U.S.N.
07/11/88 Strawberry time; about 2 weeks later than usual.
07/20/88 Repainted outside of tower and dwelling house this summer according to directions received; viz:
walls: white
trimmings: lead-color
lantern: black
Heretofore, the whole was uniformly white.
07/31/88 Inspector visited this station the second time this season. Arrived 9 A.M., departed 11 A.M. Weather fine.
08/09/88 Frost last night. The more tender vegetables such as beans and cucumbers greatly suffered from it.
08/15/88 Weather for the last two weeks has been but moderately warm and rather changeable. If anything, the summer thus far has been more remarkable for its coolness than otherwise.
08/20/88 Westerly winds for the last five days. Chimney swallows, which breed here every summer, have left their nest and departed from the island a few days ago.
August 25th and 26th were the two warmest days of the season.
09/18/88 Steam barge "Samuel Hodge" came near running aground Saturday night (15th instant) during a heavy fog. The Captain could not see the light, but fortunately heard the foghorn. The boat was within 30 or 40 rods of the light.
Stormy weather from the 16th to the 18th.

09/22/88 Inspector Comdr. H.Elmer visited this station for the third time this season. He was accompanied by Lt.House Engineer Col. Mansfield.

09/26/88 A gale from the NW with heavy rains, weather damp and stormy until close of the month

10/09/88 The first frost of the season last night.

10/19/88 A gale blowing from the NW. Rain intermixed with snow.

10/31/88 The month was very mild and (excepting the one case above) without night frosts.

The last two days (30th & 31st) were especially fine - regular Indian Summer weather.

11/20/88 The weather has been dry and mostly clear up to date. Except for a very light sprinkling a week ago, there has been no snow and the ground is entirely bare.

11/30/88 Extinguished the light for the season.

1889

04/22/89 Arrived at the station on the 22nd. Unusually early opening of navigation. Channels and Lake entirely free of ice.

04/24/89 Snowstorm. Snow melted almost as fast as it fell.

04/27/89 Some more snow intermixed with rained.

May: Weather exceedingly warm during first week and very smoky.

05/05/89 thunderstorm

05/07/89 heavy rain squalls

05/26/89 This was the first warm day after a number of rainy, or damp and very cool days. Vegetation is well-advanced. Strawberries have been in blossom for over two weeks. The leaves are well-developed, those of poplar and birch nearly full-grown. This island has ever been remarkable as the favorite habitat of rabbits, but this year there is not a single one to be found. Foxes have exterminated them. I saw as many as five together last summer. They were feeding on grasshoppers and later upon the refuse from the kitchen. Of course, they were prisoners on the island and could not escape until winter would build an ice bridge for them. I shot one of them last fall from the kitchen window; the others left during the winter or else starved to death.

06/10/89 U.S. steamer "Warrington" arrived at this station at 3 P.M. with annual supplies. Comdr. Horace Elmer, Lt.House Inspector and Col.Ludlow, Lt.House Engineer, inspected the station, leaving at 5 P.M. Everything, it seems, was found satisfactory.

06/21/89 a cold and stormy day

06/30/89 The season so far has been exceptionally free from thunder showers.

07/07/89 Atmosphere thick and hazy.

07/16/89 Sultry. The hottest day of the season.

07/25/89 A picnic party from Bayfield numbering about forty (mostly ladies and young girls) visited this station. They had intended to enjoy the day on the shores of Presque Isle, but bad and heavy weather caused them to take refuge under the roof of the Keeper`s dwelling.

08/02/89 Comdr. Horace Elmer, Inspector, called at this station 3 P.M., coming from Sand Island. Left 6 P.M. for Outer Island station. Weather cloudy.

08/31/89 This month was the warmest of the season.
Heavy rains and thunderstorms occurred on the 17th and 19th during night; foggy days on the 16th and 19th.

09/09/89 Passenger-birds are very numerous on the islands. They feed on grasshoppers and berries, especially of the wild cherry and mountain ash which are more plentiful than usual.

09/19/89 Rather heavy weather of late. Yesterday it blew a gale from the NW; today fine but decidedly cool. U.S. steamer "Warrington" passed this station yesterday afternoon on her way down, she being on her 3rd inspection trip. The storm prevented her from calling at this station.

09/21/89 A frost this morning - the first of the season - killed vegetables in garden

09/29/89 a warm and fine day

October: the weather was mild during the whole of the month.

10/21/89 Two fishermen, today, capsized their boat and drowned off York Island, the wind blowing moderately from the south.

11/24/89 The weather was exceptionally fine this month - last night we had a little sprinkling of snow - the night before the ground froze for the first time this season - the [16th-20th] may be called our Indian Summer. A steam barge passed this station today upwards bound, and may be the last boat of the season going west.

11/30/89 Extinguished the Light for the season. Left the station for the winter, by permission of the inspector.

1890

04/25/90 Arrived at the station and lit the lamp for the first time of the season. Channels almost free of ice.

05/18/90 Up-to-date, the weather has been unusually cold. Snowstorms occurred several times this month. With the exception of a faint blush of meadow green just appearing, vegetation is still dormant. This is the most belated spring within the recollection of the present writer. Ice and snow still remains in the cavities of the rocks on the north side of the island.

04/30/90 Until within a few days the weather has been as chilly as above described, but the last days of the month turned out milder, bringing with them rain and fog. The effect upon vegetation was electrical.

06/05/90 Rainstorm from the NE. Steam barge "Fisk" on her way to Duluth turned back and ran in for shelter. She laid off the station part of the night.

06/18/90 Comdr. P.F. Heyerman, U.S.N. inspected the station during my absence. A dispatch had ordered me home the week previous, my wife being seriously ill (typhoid fever).

06/30/90 Damp and foggy

The weather during the month, on an average, was genial and pleasant.

07/01/90 Damp and foggy

07/15/90 The weather thus far has been alternately dry and damp, or rainy, during this month. Vegetation has made very rapid progress. There never was as fine a crop of hay than this season since the present keeper has had the charge of this station. Fruit-bearing plants and shrubs, also, are very prolific.

07/27/90 A very warm day. Inspector O.F. Heyerman, Comdr. U.S.N. visited this station at 9 A.M. Rear Admiral D.B. Harmony was aboard the Lt. House tender "Warrington," but did not get off at this station.

08/05/90 heavy rain squall last night coming from south

08/09/90 Mr. Currie Bell, Editor of the Bayfield County Press, and family, visited the station. They were encamped on the Sand beach near boat house. This is raspberry time. Picked the first on the 3rd instant.

08/15/90 For several days not a boat passed this channel. The interruption was caused by the breakage of a valve in the locks of the canal at Sault St. Mary. The damage being repaired, boats are now coming up thickly.

08/27/90 Inspector O.F. Heyerman, Comdr. U.S.N. visited this station at 9 A.M. - his 3rd call this season.

09/06/90 Except yesterday & the day before, the week has been damp and foggy.

09/06/90 Rain, thunder & lightning A.M.

09/17-24/90

Raining weather with thunder & lightning.

The month ends very fine.

11/30/90 Extinguished the light for the season and left for Bayfield during a snowstorm. With the exception of the 15th, the weather was very dry from the 10th until the end of the month.

This photo was taken after additions in 1906-1907 brought the Raspberry Island Lighthouse close to its present appearance.

Chapter Thirteen
Lighthouse People: Bits and Pieces Around the Archipelago

In six years of visiting Apostle Islands lighthouses, and three years of active research, it is possible to gather lots of interesting stories that do not really fit anywhere, but still are worth telling.

Below are some of those stories, as told by Apostle Islands lighthouse people.

Robert Brander knew his father worked on lighthouses in Lake Superior, St. Mary's River and Lake Huron from 1922 to 1948. But Brander, who still lives in the Apostle Islands area, was not aware of how close his work place was to that of his father, Thomas Brander. Here is the odd way he found out.

I never knew that my father was at Outer Island. I worked for the Apostle Islands National Lakeshore as ecologist for several years, directing the research program, and spent a lot of time staying at Outer Island Light when we were doing work out there, research projects. And I slept on the second floor in one of the bedrooms. After several years, the historian at Apostle Islands was looking through the log for Outer Island. And there was an entry on a given day in 1926, "Thomas Brander arrived today." I then learned that he was the first occupant of what is the third floor.

From the entries, Robert Brander learned that his father arrived at Outer Island in August 1926, where he served as third assistant for the rest of the year. Brander believes his father was the first third assistant ever to serve at Outer Island. Thus, he may have been the first occupant of the then-new third floor quarters.

I had slept there many a night lying on the second floor, looking at the ceiling, never knowing that sixty years before that, my father was the occupant. . . . It was a non-experience when it was happening. It was only in retrospect that the full impact comes on me.

Here Brander talks about an unusual plant species found nowhere else in Wisconsin but the north shore of Devils Island, where his father once paid a visit to his friend, Devils Island Keeper Hans Christensen. It is a grasslike plant, called a sedge, known only in Iceland.

The theory we have is that the Coast Guard brought in a bulldozer to rebuild the road that runs the length of Devils Island. . . . And we got the serial number off that Caterpillar tractor that was used, and it had been used in the construction of Thule Air Force Base in Greenland. There's a chance that sedge would also be in Greenland. . . . The seeds (probably) came in the dirt that was embedded in the tractor. But that's hypothesis. . . .

Devils was entirely a lighthouse reservation, so other than the road that was put in to connect the boat house with the light station, it's really a virgin forest, as is Raspberry Island. It wasn't logged, therefore. . . . We've aged some of the (white pines on Devils Island). . . .Those trees, some of them, are in excess of four-hundred years old.

From 1992 to 1998, visitors to Raspberry Island knew Matt Welter as freeliving Herbert "Toots" Winfield. Welter played the part of Winfield, who served as an assistant at Raspberry Island during the 1920s.

Although Welter injected humor into many of his portrayals of Winfield, he also used some of his stories to show the dangers of life at a lighthouse.

In one of his presentations, he told about the care needed to light a kerosene lamp.

You want to have as little oil up in the tower with that precious lens as possible. . . . The kerosene would be sent through a sand filter. You'd just essentially have a filtered ring that they could pour the kerosene through. . . . It would be (done) down in the fuel house. You want to keep as much of the explosive material as possible down in the fuel house. Part of the reason why, and this is what I tell people as Toots, is because, think about it, you've got a magnifying glass in here. . . . You could focus it down on there just like a magnifying glass. Boom! The whole thing would go and so would the lens. . . .

The only time you bring it up to the light is half an hour before sunset and you take it out half an hour after sunrise, just after you blow it out. . . .

What I would tell people is that you would light the light from Raspberry when the sun was about four fingers off the horizon. And keepers would use little systems like that to keep them going. Your lighthouse might be high enough that you only use two fingers up, or

During the 1990s, Matt Welter played the part of Herbert "Toots" Winfield, a free-living assistant keeper at the Raspberry Island Lighthouse in the 1920s.

you might be two hands high. It just depends on where you're at, what your lighthouse is like and what the land situation is. But at Raspberry, it was four fingers up. . . .

The keepers out at Raspberry would put a mirror on a pedestal out and angle it up at the light so they could watch it from their living room, just periodically keep watch on it. But if it was a drafty night, you'd have to be up there all the time. If it was raining, you'd have to be up there all the time. . .

Experiences Welter and his wife had at Devils Island showed him some of the problems keepers and their families had on islands.

Devils Island has one of the most interesting fly populations in the world. I have stayed at Devils a couple nights, and one of the things that impressed me about the fly population is we had three days of rain, no problem, and then the fly hatch came. And these are cluster flies. They like to cluster up. And there were mixed in there biting flies as well. But the flies, if I was wearing a white pair of pants, which I was at the time, would cover my pants completely. . . . .You could get it to the point where they'd start to form a little ball on your legs.

You could actually get it to about the size of a croquet ball and knock it off. And you could actually kick it around if you want. I'm not kidding you. . . .

If you wanted to get the flies off of you before running into the house, you could literally run around the house, my wife and I did this. We ran both directions and passed each other and as we passed each other, it was like watching a Yogi Bear cartoon. You'd see you go by and then this cluster of flies following right after you.

Lighthouses in the Apostle Islands were sometimes places of deep faith, as the Rev. R.B. Howard found while he was on a summer vacation in the area in the early 1870s. Here, the Lutheran minister from Chicago describes what happened when he encountered Raspberry Island Light Station Keeper Lars Larson at the nearby Indian agency of Red Cliff:

I found on inquiring that he kept the U.S. Lighthouse on Raspberry Island, fifteen miles from Bayfield, Wisconsin. He was a devout Swedish Lutheran and was returning in his boat from market with his two months' supplies.

In answer to my queries he told me of his wife's faith and life, and closed by asking if I would not go off with him to the place where, for five years, no minister had been, and administer the rite of baptism to his little Hilda and Jonas; . . . Well, I went with him bowled along by a spanking breeze. We saw the light that his wife Annie (the assistant keeper) had kindled as soon as the sun went down. He glanced at me cheerfully. His forty-eight hours' absence made him fear a little, but the light reassured him of the safety of his dear ones.

Howard wrote how the moon was up by the time the vessel grazed the white sand of the sand spit that then was next to the boathouse.

Annie came down three-fourths of a mile through a wood path, to meet the boat that the setting sun had shown her scudding across the bay. She gave the . . . stranger a cordial welcome, as a few confidential Swedish phrases revealed his offices and errand. After the boat was hauled up, you should have seen our procession thro' the woods and over the fallen trees, out to the clearing on the point where Hilda and Jonas were sweetly sleeping under the kindly flashing of the light. The minister led, bearing a package of groceries, then came Lars with a bag on his back and a lantern in his hand, and then Annie, not unburdened, for Swedes are importing the right of women to labor out of doors. We had to look well to our feet, and were glad when the breakers on the shore told us we were near the point where the tower with its beacon rose from the center of a substantial house.

After a hearty supper, a stroll by moonlight, and a look at a . . . steamer, I retired to a chamber, (through) the opposite window of which fell the light of the moon and of an aurora borealis, the interspersing rays of which were uninterrupted save by a bedstead and chair, the entire furniture of the apartment.

But when I had stretched myself on the clean bed of straw between the windows, and thought of Him who does not like to sleep; it seemed to me, for a moment, like lying in the light between two angels in the ark of the covenant, and I thought of little ones other than the flaxen-haired babes below. . . . The next morning was clear and bright and when the breakfast cloth was removed, Lars and Annie, dressed becomingly, presented their babes, with grateful tears, while I, after extemporaneous cathechizing and address, baptized them in the name of the Father, Son and Holy Ghost. They showed me a well-worn Swede English Testament. They never omitted family prayer or a verse at the table. By and by they must go off the island and send the children to school, but their first reading must be the word of God.

Apostle Islands National Lakeshore
An assistant keeper, some children and an owl pose in front of the keeper's quarters at the Devils Island Light Station in the first part of the twentieth century.

Chapter Fourteen
Randall Peterson: Spotlighting Lighthouses With Little Dots

Somewhere in the possessions of Mikhail Gorbachev is a print of the skyline of St. Paul, Minn., done by Randall J. Peterson.

The fact that the late Minnesota Gov. Rudy Perpich chose a print by Peterson as a gift for the former Soviet leader is an indication of the artist's ability, and of the range of his work.

Indeed, Peterson can choose lots of subjects. But he's settled on a specialty of lighthouses, as the subjects of his pen-and-ink prints painstakingly done in the pointillism process used by French artist Georges Pierre Seurat.

The Forest Lake, Minn. resident is in the midst of following his love of lighthouses and his avocation as a pointillist artist, by doing a series of lighthouse pictures, ranging from the Lime Kiln Lighthouse on San Juan Island in Washington State to Amelia Island in Florida.

The Apostle Islands are well represented in that group. In the spring of 2001, Peterson was finishing work on a picture of the LaPointe Light Station, after doing representations of the other five stations of the Apostle Islands National Lakeshore.

"This gives me the opportunity to travel, visit with the volunteers that work at these lighthouses, learn about their historical significance, do my photography work, do thumbnail sketches," said Peterson, who pursues his outside work as an artist, while keeping a full-time job as an electronic prepress supervisor.

"I started off by doing cityscapes around the Twin Cities area, small towns around the Twin Cities area, mainly structures, historic points of interest," said Peterson.

The focus shifted after he did his first lighthouse in 1991, at Split Rock, on the Northern Shore of Lake Superior, in Minnesota.

"Lighthouses to me, working with this particular style, lends itself to the structures, to the landscapes, trees, rocks, things of that nature," Peterson said.

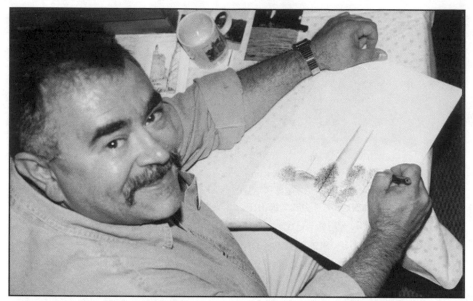

Randall Peterson works on his print of the Outer Island Lighthouse. Four of his other Apostle Islands lighthouse prints are pictured in this chapter.

To Peterson, going back to places where there are boats, ships and - of course - lighthouses - is a draw.

"I've read about lighthouses, the deterioration of lighthouses. To me I do feel that there is a need for an awareness of these lighthouses," Peterson said. "The meaning of lighthouses themselves I find very intriguing."

Peterson adopted his process of artwork about the same time he did his first lighthouse.

"Back in the eighties, I did a lot of pencil drawings for Sears. . . . pencil illustrations, ink illustrations," he said. He changed his style around 1990. "I went to pen-and-ink drawings."

The process, also called stippling, is not an easy one.

"There's not a whole lot of people that do it, and I think that's because of the patience that it takes to do it. It takes a long time to do it. There's no way that I can get the true value out of my originals because of the fact that it takes so long to do," said Peterson.

In September 1999, he was spending a couple of days doing his work and greeting customers at the Keeper of the Light lighthouse and nautical gift store in Bayfield, during the Fourth Annual Apostle Islands Lighthouse Celebration.

"This one will take about forty hours," he said, pointing to a partially completed print of the Outer Island Lighthouse. "It's a process where you can only work on it probably two or three hours at a time. Then you've got to get away from it, because you're working so close that you start to maybe shade in areas where you don't want to shade," Peterson said.

Sand Island Lighthouse

"Generally what I do with these lighthouses, I'll get out to the locations. There's been one case where I had a friend shoot one for me out on the East Coast there. I didn't get a chance to get to that one. Otherwise, they're my own photography work. I try to do thumbnail sketches while I'm out there, because a lot of times. . . . your eyes can pick up a lot more than what the film can pick up."

Although Peterson specializes in lighthouses, he also does other work, including collections from Minnesota and New England. Some of his projects include commissioned illustrations of the Whitney Hotel in Minneapolis, Minn. and the Holiday Inn Hotels.

Peterson's artwork is represented in China, Germany, India, Japan, Norway and Sweden. While Peterson does various kinds of work, his primary focus remains lighthouses, a pursuit that has brought him to locations throughout the country.

For the Outer Island print, Peterson took a picture from a boat that passed close by, on a trip where he had hoped to get to the shore. "I didn't get a chance to get on shore. The waves were too big."

Among the others he has done are Two Harbors and Duluth South Harbor in Minnesota; Fort Niagara, Buffalo Main and Tibbetts Point in New York State; Chicago Harbor in Illinois; and Cape Hatteras and Cape Lookout in North Carolina.

Peterson has 975 prints made of each original, all numbered and signed by the artist. Then he keeps the pen used in creating the artwork with the original, so they can be sold as a package.

"I'm getting a lot of requests from the East Coast," he said. "Essentially I started out. I selected thirty lighthouses I'm going to do. With the response from my e-mail, I could easily do another thirty."

"My hope is that the series will raise public awareness about lighthouses and prevent them from becoming extinct," Peterson wrote in a brochure. "I selected the thirty lighthouses represented in my series because they convey a powerful sense of place - some located in stunningly beautiful remote areas and others anchored securely in the hearts of the communities they serve."

There is not only business in Peterson's trips to the islands.

"Two years ago, my wife and I went to Niagara Falls. From there, that's where we took a trip to Tibbetts Point, which is on Lake Ontario, at the mouth of the St. Lawrence Seaway. That was a trip where we would stop at three or four lighthouses a day. The photography work, just visiting with the different volunteers. Just incredible," Peterson said.

"There's no way I could sit there for forty hours with the weather and the elements and draw that particular light station or lighthouse. It's great," Peterson said.

Although there's work in the trips, Peterson considers it a break from the intensity of his full-time job.

Devils Island Light Station

"Even though it's lighthouses, and we're eventually going to be doing something with them, to us it's still a vacation," Peterson said. "My wife, she enjoys the lighthouses just as much as we do." Their son, Andrew, and daughter, Kristine, also sometimes come along.

Wherever he goes, or wherever he gets his pictures, Peterson is impressed by the way the lights operated in a simpler technology.

"How could they construct something like that back in those days.....The way they had to put them together, how they got these parts up on these cliffs to build these lighthouses. You're talking mid-to-late 1800s," Peterson said. "These structures have outlived buildings in cities."

Others looking at him at work are impressed by the way Peterson does his artwork.

"It's all little dots. Even the solid areas are created by dots," he said, talking with Ann Lanich. An elementary school teacher from Wausaukee, Wisc., Lanich spoke to Peterson while he was at the Keeper of the Light gift shop during the Apostle Islands Lighthouse Celebration.

"I'm quite impressed with his work. That's what I came up to see," said Lanich, who does water color, and wanted to talk with Peterson about what he does. "I love your work."

When Lanich left, she brought a pack of Peterson's lightcards, with his autograph.

She also had placed a few dots on Peterson's Outer Island print. Those who buy the print will also get a bonus. They'll see, in an inconspicuous corner of that picture, dots placed by a certain writer who interviewed Peterson one September day in Bayfield.

Raspberry Island Lighthouse

Michigan Island Light Station

Chapter Fifteen
An Unexpected Visitor:
A Short Story

(The following story is from *Black Island*, a yet-to-be-published novel by the author. It is based on the Devils Island Light Station.)

On a midnight watch at the top of a lighthouse on an island in Lake Superior, a first assistant keeper found a moment of stillness when there was no clockwork to wind, no passing ship to watch and no storm on the way. In that free moment, he stood by a window with a pen in his hand and a diary before him. By the light from the lens in the lantern room above, he began to write.

Wednesday, July 11, 1928
Dear Diary,
I sense a stirring on this watch, which came from reading the Book of Revelation.
He is coming soon. No one knows the day or the hour. But he is surely coming. He cometh on a day we do not expect. He cometh as a thief in the night. There will be weeping and gnashing of teeth for all who are not ready. He could come any time. He could come with the dawn.
Yours until then,
Samuel Clemens Brown
First Assistant Keeper
Black Island Light Station

Four hours later, the wife of Samuel Clemens Brown sat with her two children on a rock on the northeast landing of Black Island, waiting for the sunrise to break through the morning fog. Louise Brown turned to her right and noticed for the thousandth time how the blond hair of her daughter, Abbie, matched her own. Then she turned to George, and considered once again how his dark puppy-dog eyes resembled his Papa's. Even with the intermittent blaring of the foghorn, there was a peacefulness about times like this, that never seemed to end.
"Do you hear something, Abbie?" George asked.
"Yes, dummy. It's the foghorn. It's foggy."
"No, listen. It's a different sound," George said.

The sound seemed to come from the direction of the sun itself. It was a humming noise, heard between the whines of the foghorn. The sunrise was bigger, and so was the noise from the east. Louise stood up.

"It's the inspector's boat," she said. "He could come any time. But he came with the dawn."

Now everything happened at once. The fog was quickly lifting, and the lighthouse tender was in sight. The foghorn was off, which meant Louise, Abbie and George could hear the sound of the tender clearly.

Three times, a bell sounded from the light tower. In response, the approaching vessel blew its whistle three times. "George, Abbie. We've got to get back to the house," Louise said. They ran all the way back on the path to their quarters. When they arrived, Louise saw Papa dashing out the door, while he buttoned his uniform.

Keeper McClatchy hurried from his quarters and stood in front of the house where the Browns lived. He met Papa, who had just exited the house. "It's an old trick, coming right up to us with the sunrise, so we don't see the inspector until the last minute," the keeper said. "Did you mop the floor of the foghorn building yesterday, Sam, like I told you to do?"

"Yes Al, I did."

"You'll hear from me if you didn't."

"Papa's got a black sock on one foot, and a gray sock on the other," Abbie said to George.

George rushed to his room and threw his picture of the 1926 St. Louis Cardinals into a drawer. He did the dusting he'd neglected and swept the floor. The shooshing sound of a straw broom on the hardwood floor came up the stairs. "Mother's not going to pick up anything," Abbie said from her room. "She swept up three times yesterday, and mopped once."

Soon, Abbie and George were back in the kitchen, staring up to Mother for instructions.

"Go down to the Gundersen's shanty, and stay there until I come for you. Tell Rose the inspector's here. She'll fix you breakfast," Mother said, while she opened the door for George and Abbie to walk out. "If you stay around here, you'll just be in the way."

The children rushed toward the trail leading to the southern end of the island and the Gundersen's shanty.

A short time later, George watched as Rose Gundersen placed two more bowls of oatmeal on her table, near bowls in front of her two children, Joey and Mollie.

"Eat up, Abbie and George. It's good to have company for a day. It gets lonely down here, especially when Mr. Gundersen goes out on the fishing boat," Mrs. Gundersen said. "When you're done, you four can go out and play. Come back at lunch time and stay out of trouble."

Ignoring Mrs. Gundersen's admonition to stay out of trouble, Abbie, George, Joey and Mollie scampered out the house and up the trail. Soon, they were back at the edge of the lighthouse reservation on their bellies behind trees. In this hiding place, they saw Keeper McClatchy, Papa and Jake, the second assistant, by the foghorn building, talking with another man they'd never seen before. He was skinny and short and covered with wrinkles. He removed his cap, and revealed a head without a hair. He scratched the top of that head and placed the cap back on.

The man looked down at Papa's feet and raised his eyebrows. "Interesting choice of socks," he said.

"Yes, Inspector Olafson," Papa said.

"That guy's face looks like a raisin," Joey whispered.

"Be quiet. They'll hear us," Abbie said.

"I can't stand these flies," George whispered.

"Hold still," Abbie whispered in George's ear. "He's headed this way."

Indeed he was. Inspector Olafson was walking directly toward the foursome. George was convinced he was looking into his eyes.

"There's something in those trees," the inspector said. "No, I was wrong. There's nothing here at all. Now why don't you three wait here, while I inspect the foghorn building?"

The inspector seemed to be inside the foghorn building all afternoon. At last, though, he emerged, holding a bucket and a mop in his hands.

"Does anyone know how this came to be on the floor, in front of the foghorn machinery?"

Papa's face turned red. "I think I left it there."

"You idiot," Mr. McClatchy said. "Don't you know you're supposed to put things away when you're finished? First you put on those mismatched socks. Now you did this. Can't you do anything right? I should fire you right now."

Papa sat on a bench on the outside of the foghorn building while the keeper continued his tirade. George turned his head to the right, and saw Mother on a chair on the porch of the Browns' quarters. Her head was in her hands, and her hair appeared strangely limp.

Keeper McClatchy stopped when the inspector placed his hand on Mr. McClatchy's shoulder. "We can talk about that later," he said.

Inspector Olafson led the three keepers of the Black Island Light Station to the first assistant's quarters. He pulled a fresh pair of white gloves from a pocket and looked in the direction of the children once more. For the first time that day, a grin came over his face, right before he went inside the house with the others.

As soon as they were able, the four children were up and running and didn't stop until they were halfway to the Gundersen shanty.

"He howls at the moon," Joey said, between pants. "He'll be back tonight to eat us."

"Did you hear what Mr. McClatchy said to Papa?" George said, gasping for breath.

"Yes," Abbie said. "That's why he's mean Mr. McClatchy."

The children ran all the way back to the Gundersens' shanty and stayed there until Mother returned late in the afternoon. When she arrived, George noticed there was none of the normal glow in her eyes.

"It's time to go back," Mother said, mumbling. "Inspector Olafson's gone."

"Did Papa do OK, Mother?" George said.

"It was bad. The inspector noticed your Papa's mismatched socks. Then he discovered a bucket and mop on the floor of the foghorn building, right where your Papa left it."

"Really?" George said. He was trying as hard as he could to sound surprised.

"Mr. McClatchy kept yelling at your Papa, telling him everything he's ever done wrong," Mother said. "Now that the inspector's gone, Keeper McClatchy isn't saying anything. He's just stewing."

Two hours later, Papa, Mother, George and Abbie sat at the dining room table, eating supper without a word. Papa broke the silence, just as Mother brought out the last course, raspberry pie.

"Did he have to crucify me, just because I left that bucket and mop out in the foghorn building?" Papa asked, his words breaking. "What did he expect when I woke up with two hours' sleep? Of course, I'll put on one black sock and one gray sock."

"I know, dear. I know."

"That clockwork that turns the lamp was a mess when I first came to Black Island this spring. And that compressed air diaphone foghorn hasn't worked right since they got it three years ago. Neither has the radio fog beacon. I fixed `em all, right after I came this spring. They're running like a top."

"I know dear."

"Ships in fog can tell how far they are from the island by counting the time between when they hear the sound on the radio and when they hear the diaphone. But if they don't work right, they can't tell anything. If I hadn't been here to fix `em, they would have had to bring in a repairman."

"I know, Sam. You made them run as good as new."

The four family members were finishing the last of that pie when they observed through a window Mr. McClatchy walking toward the quarters and up the stairs to the front porch. He was in the uniform he wore on the dressiest of occasions and was carrying a tray that held what he normally served only to guests on the island. There was a pitcher of his special apple-flavored punch and a bowl of his ginger-flavored cookies. Also on the tray were four glasses and a paper sack.

The tray and everything on it were shaking.

"May I come in?" he asked through an open window. "I can't stay long. My watch starts soon, and I've got to get the light lit."

"The door's not locked," Mother said. "Children, why don't you go upstairs?"

"No, they need to hear this too," Mr. McClatchy said.

George fiddled with his hands, and noticed everyone was doing the same.

"Have some punch and cookies. I made them for all of you."

"Yes sir," Abbie said. Nobody ate anything.

"Inspector Olafson had a long talk with me before he left. He was upset. But not with you, Sam."

"He wasn't?" Papa said.

"No. He was upset with me. He said I was wrong to berate you the way I did, in front of other people. He insisted that I apologize to the whole family, because the whole family was present. So I'm apologizing."

"Then we'll have to accept it," Mother said. "But Abbie and George weren't there."

"Apparently, they were. Inspector Olafson said he spotted two boys and two girls hiding in the woods when I yelled at you, Sam. He was going to say something, but didn't."

Mother turned her face toward the children. "We'll have to talk about that later, Abbie, George."

"The inspector said he would of course have to make note of the bucket and the mop he found on the floor of the foghorn building. He also would make a notation that you were wearing one black sock and one gray sock when you met the inspector."

"That's only right," Papa said. "I could give a reason for both of these. But there's really no excuse."

"But he also said he'd make much longer notations about the condition of the clockwork, the compressed air diaphone foghorn and the radio fog beacon. He said in 20 years as a lighthouse inspector, he's never seen machinery in as good condition as he found it here. He said that more than makes up for the mop and bucket and socks."

"He did?" said Papa, his face suddenly brighter.

"Not only that, he thinks you're a genius with machinery, and that the Lighthouse Service is lucky to have you."

"I'm starting to like Inspector Olafson," Mother said.

"He also said he never found a family's quarters as clean as he found yours," the keeper said. "He didn't find any dust anywhere."

"I am a keeper's daughter, after all," Mother said. "I do know how to keep things clean."

"He also said he found a large amount of dust on top of the door into my bedroom," the keeper said. "I thought I'd cleaned that. But obviously, I didn't."

"Oh," Mother said.

Mr. McClatchy reached into his pocket and pulled out an envelope. "I have a letter for you, George and Abbie. It's also for the two junior fishermen at the bottom of this island. Would you like me to read it?"

"I think we'd like that," Mother said.

"To my four little friends under the trees:

"You probably think I'm quite mean, the way I go about the island with such a cross face and manner. I do it because lives and ships could be lost if the Lighthouse Service doesn't do its job right. That's why the service insists that everything is done properly here.

"You remind me of my four grandchildren in Detroit. I bought some candy for them in the candy store in Duluth. But the way you were laying down flat in the middle of the trees made me think of the way they look when we are playing hide-and-seek. I pretend not to see them, either.

"That's why I've decided to leave the candy here for the four of you. You were the bright spot of the old man's day. The next time I surprise you with a visit. I'll bring some more.

"Your friend, Michael Olafson, Inspector, U.S. Lighthouse Service.

"P.S.: The next time I'm here, don't be so shy."

George saw Keeper McClatchy reach into the sack that had been on the tray. He brought out four smaller sacks. "This is the candy Inspector Olafson was talking about," he said. "One is for you, Abbie, and one is for you, George. I believe the other two sacks are for Joey and Mollie Gundersen."

George thought he saw moisture in Papa's eyes, and a tear on Mother's cheek. Before he could get a close view of the keeper's eyes, Mr. McClatchy walked out the door, leaving the tray with the cookies and punch behind.

July 11, 1928

Dear Diary:

I have just read the entry I made in you less than 24 hours ago. I feared that he would come, and he came. I just didn't say who "he" was!

What gnashing of teeth would have awaited us, if we were not ready.

Yours,

Sam

Under a sky filled with bright pinholes, George sat with Papa and Mother and Abbie on a rock at the very northern end of the island. Before them was a wonder greater than George had ever seen.

"There's blues and oranges and greens," George said. "It's got to be angel hair."

"No, dummy, angels don't get that big," Abbie said. "That's the drapes of the mansion God's making for us in heaven."

"You're both wrong," Papa said. "Scientists give all kinds of reasons why we got this second unexpected visitor of the day. That may explain how the Northern Lights got there. But it doesn't say who made it happen."

"God, Papa?" George said.

"Yes, God. He's saying how great he is."

"Papa, is this how it's going to look when Jesus comes back?" George said.

"No, George, it'll look much bigger and brighter. Everybody in the world will see it, not just us way up far north."

"Do you know when he'll come?"

"No, I don't, George. But when this unexpected visitor comes, we'll have even less notice than we did for Inspector Olafson."

Afterword
The Heart of a Keeper

I was on top of a continent, where I could see with turns of my neck where water flows into the Pacific, and where it meanders into the Atlantic. In this first sightseeing vacation in years that didn't include a visit to a lighthouse, my mind said the view on the Trail Ridge Road of the Rocky Mountain National Park was spectacular.

But inside, my heart told me something was missing. Where was the surf and the spray that comes on a boat on the way to an island? Above all, where were the light towers, signaling to the mariners?

Most people standing on a mountain 12,000 feet above sea level would never understand that sense. But for those with the heart of a keeper, it's too real.

It wasn't long ago that I thought lighthouses were corny. To me, people who had pictures of lighthouses on a wall were the same ones who had velvet pictures of Elvis on another wall.

Now I write frequently on the topic. I'm writing a novel about a family at a lighthouse, and telling stories about them before audiences.

One Christmas, my sister gave me a lighthouse calendar, my in-laws got me a lighthouse picture and my wife handed me a lighthouse book. It's clear I'm hooked.

So what's changed? Me, of course. I've grown older. I've learned more about the noble profession of keeper. And I've spent time at lighthouses.

There's more to lighthouses than corn. There are words that stir the heart. Words like danger and beauty. Loneliness has a place in this dictionary of words attached to lighthouses, as does bravery. Add to this solace, direction and safety.

Some people look to the hills, whence their help comes, for the connection to what's inside. But I'll stay close to the waters, where there's a light in a tower nearby.

I'm not alone.

True, I've come to realize it's best not to bore people with everything I know about how they moved the Cape Hatteras Lighthouse, whenever someone says, "I like lighthouses."

I know what it means, when most people say that. They are the dabblers, who see the hard core among us as fanatics.

But even the dabblers have the basics within them.

Far from any ocean, a look inside any big city phone book tells the story. There's always a church or two whose name includes the name lighthouse.

Religions may differ widely, but it seems a common theme is the use of the word light to mean a sentinel that directs one away from darkness and danger, and in the right direction.

"O send out Thy light and Thy truth: let them lead me," the 43rd Psalm declares. "And the light shineth in darkness; and the darkness comprehended it not," says the opening of the Book of John, in a description of Jesus. "I am the light of the world," Jesus said more than once, in the Book of John.

There is as well in the Good Book a description of when there will be no more danger, and people no longer need sentinels.

"And there shall be no night there; and they need no candle, neither light of the sun; for the Lord God giveth them light: and they shall reign for ever and ever," says the last chapter of the Book of Revelation.

One needn't be religious to feel the need for the direction that light brings. "Give light and the people will find their own way," says the slogan of the media giant E.W. Scripps Co. Publisher Carl Magee first used it on the masthead of his Albuquerque, N.M., newspaper in 1922. Magee also used a picture of a lighthouse as a logo for his column "Turning on the Light." When Scripps acquired Magee's paper, it used the logo and motto as its own.

There's plenty of symbolism in a lighthouse. But it doesn't take a theologian or a newspaper publisher to appreciate the stories told about lighthouses, or the mariners whose lives they saved.

And anyone with eyes can appreciate their beauty.

Lighthouses went up in places that already were breathtaking. If there were no lighthouses at Cape Hatteras, Montauk Point or Point Reyes, people would still visit there and remark on the beauty of the places. By placing architectural wonders in the midst of these places, lighthouse builders created focal points, and complete scenes worthy of El Greco, Monet, Rembrant or Guichard. Lighthouses go in the spot where you would pose a couple for a wedding picture, or perhaps a lovely lady in an evening gown, seated on a boulder, and gazing into the distance.

Anybody can see that. But only the initiated really appreciate what went on inside the lighthouses themselves.

Consider the technical marvels that lighthouse keepers of years past performed, before electricity, computers or satellite systems that now enable anyone with a cheap device to determine position within several hundred feet. Imagine. The captain of a ship traveling at night during the nineteenth century could determine his general position, as long as he was within sight of a lighthouse that gave the same characteristic signal.

If he saw at the same time another characteristic signal from a second lighthouse, he could determine by triangulation his position in the water with great accuracy. It may not have been as accurate as the global positioning systems of today, but it was more than adequate to keep him away from the rocks and headed toward home.

Two pictures of the spiral staircase of the Outer Island Light tower placed side-by-side create a spinning sensation.

And what were the signals from those lights? Flashes of light, either white or another color, that repeated every so many seconds. It's easy to do that today, with automated solar-powered beacons. But they did it in an age that was just beginning to discover the uses of electricity. They did it with painstakingly-maintained mechanical clockwork that turned a meticulously cleaned collection of prisms and lenses assembled so that every bit of light inside pointed the same way, perhaps dozens of miles away.

The source of that light wasn't electricity, but lanterns no more complicated than the ones Scouts bring on camping trips today.

At the beginning of the twenty-first century, this technology is ancient. But it worked, because of the craftsmanship that went into it, and the dedication of the keepers that kept those lights burning, often under impossible conditions.

These were people with stories to tell.

A favorite is Abbie Burgess, the brave teenager who kept the light burning at an island light station in Maine when her father was stuck on the shore in a winter storm. Another is George Worthylake, the first keeper of the Boston Lighthouse, the first in the colonies. I liked them so much that I've used their names as the first and middle names of the two mischievous keepers' kids in my lighthouse novel.

But the acclaim doesn't go only to the keepers and keepers' families who catch the fancy of writers. There are few lighthouses that don't have their tales of bravery by those who served there. Rarer are the stories about keepers who failed in their duties.

"The lightkeepers have repeatedly shown that they are in truth 'faithful guardians,' regardless of region or race," George Putnam, the longtime commissioner of the Bureau of Lighthouses, wrote in his autobiography, *Sentinel of the Coast*. Putnam acquired a reputation as an efficient, no-nonsense leader of the nation's keepers before he retired in 1935.

In his autobiography, Putnam recounts numerous instances of their bravery and faithfulness.

"When being removed to the hospital, fatally burned in the line of duty, a native Hawaiian lightkeeper gave this parting injunction to his wife: "Stand by the 'kukui' (light) and keep it burning," Putnam writes, recounting one of those instances.

Few keepers had to give their lives for the lights. Most spent their careers holding to the endless routine of maintenance that the Lighthouse Service demanded.

The way that routine and that life changed them adds to the charm of lighthouses.

Something about living at a lighthouse set people apart, in a way I don't fully understand. There seems to be a gentleness in the keepers I've read about, and in the keepers' kids I've encountered.

This has been the view approaching the Michigan Island Light Station, ever since the erection of a new light tower in 1929.

Consider Lois Spangle, whose father served from the late 1930s to 1951 at light stations in the Apostle Islands.

"Mother Nature provided me with many entertainments and toys," she said, giving particular mention to her collections of butterflies and wildflowers. It's a great life, I will say. I'm happy with my heritage."

It's easy to speculate on the source of the gentleness that people like Lois Spangle exhibit, long after they've moved away from lighthouses. The families of keepers never got away from the sound of the surf, except when they went into town. Living in isolation, keepers' children grew closer to their parents and to each other than they possibly would in the outside world. The way their parents taught them is a showcase example of how homeschooling works. The regimen of the life, with the constant fear of visits by white-gloved inspectors looking for dust on top of window sills, internalized a self-discipline they would hold to the rest of their lives.

Although there was no time for idleness, the setting gave them a contemplative heart that few children today possess. They grew up away from television, but perhaps with a radio. Nature gave them toys.

People may debate the meaning of family values. But the life these people lived showed the ideal in family life. At the age when children today fill themselves with images of murder and sex on television, and spend hours in front of computer screens fighting aliens, they sat on beaches, reading books brought by a lighthouse tender. There, they developed the heart of the keeper.

The picture, of course, is idealized. There are stories of people who hated the life. And there are tales of those who live on mountains far from the sea, that are as attractive as anything anyone can tell about life at a light. On our visit to the Rockies, our innkeeper told us how he and his wife were caught up in the busy life of the city, and chucked it all to move their family closer to nature. I know he'll never go back. When it's time for his vacations, a co-worker heads west with his wife, and another chance to walk in the mountains. He always comes back refreshed.

Perhaps there is something in their upbringing that puts the mountains in their hearts, and made them sources of life. Indeed, there is beauty and there is symbolism in many places.

As for me, and all other keepers, our hearts will be anyplace by a body of water, where there's a beacon nearby.

Better than anyone, we understand the words of Connie Scovill Small, in her autobiography, *The Lighthouse Keeper's Wife.*

"Never in my dreams as a child and young person did I ever think I would be a lighthouse keeper's wife and live in lighthouses for twenty-eight years," wrote Small, who lived at lighthouses in Maine from 1920 to 1948. "Now, I never see a light shining from those beacons

Boaters passing by the northern end of Devils Island see sea caves undercutting the island, keepers' quarters and the light tower of the Devils Island Light Station.

but I am filled with a sense of peace and security, a sense of the trust that has gladdened the hearts of sailors all over the world for more than two thousand years."

There may be no lighthouses in heaven. But until I get there, I'll keep on keeping the light here.

Lois Spangle records for posterity her memories of life as the daughter of an Apostle Islands lightkeeper. Anne Tubiolo (with mike) and Michele Hartley were working on a new film for the Apostle Islands National Lakeshore Visitor Center.

A motorboat speeds by the Chequamegon Point Light, at the northwestern end of Long Island.

115

The view from the light tower of the Devils Island Light Station includes the station's two brick residences.

Gardens still grow at the Raspberry Island Light Station, just as they did when the station was manned.

The Sand Island Lighthouse as seen from below.

From this camera angle, the old Michigan Island Lighthouse appears to eclipse the sun.

The Fresnel lens from the old and new Michigan Island light towers is a popular attraction at the Apostle Islands National Lakeshore Visitor Center in Bayfield, Wisc.